PONS

Verben und Zeiten trainieren
ENGLISCH

In 200 Übungen Verbformen richtig bilden
und sicher anwenden.
Für Anfänger (A1) und Fortgeschrittene (B2)

von
Christina Cott

PONS GmbH
Stuttgart

PONS

Verben und Zeiten trainieren
ENGLISCH

In 200 Übungen Verbformen richtig bilden und sicher anwenden.

von
Christina Cott

Auflage A1 4 3 2 1 / 2018 2017 2016 2015

Redaktion: Brian Melican
Logoentwurf: Erwin Poell, Heidelberg
Logoüberarbeitung: Sabine Redlin, Ludwigsburg
Titelfoto: Vlado Golub, Stuttgart
Einbandgestaltung: Anne Helbich, Stuttgart
Satz: tebitron gmbh, Gerlingen
Druck und Bindung: Print Consult GmbH, München

Printed in EU
ISBN: 978-3-12-562759-8

Mit **PONS Verben und Zeiten trainieren ENGLISCH** können Sie in kleinen Portionen und wo immer Sie wollen Ihre Grammatikkenntnisse trainieren und festigen oder auffrischen. Dabei erfahren Sie auch das Wichtigste zu den Themen, die Sie üben möchten.

Verbformen bilden und richtig benutzen

Das Buch besteht aus zwei großen Bereichen:

Teil 1 beschäftigt sich mit der Formenbildung – hier üben Sie, wie man Verben richtig konjugiert und wie man bestimmte Verbkonstruktionen und Zeitformen korrekt bildet.

Teil 2 befasst sich mit dem Verb im Satz – hier trainieren Sie, Verben innerhalb eines Satzes richtig einzusetzen und die passende Zeit zu wählen.

Von leicht bis schwer

Die Übungen sind nach Grammatikthemen sortiert, damit Sie gezielt nach Ihren persönlichen Bedürfnissen üben können. Zu jedem Grammatikthema stehen Ihnen Übungen in drei Schwierigkeitsstufen zur Verfügung:

* = leicht

** = mittelschwer

*** = schwer

Unterstützung für Ihr Grammatikwissen

Am Anfang jedes Kapitels finden Sie eine Einstiegsseite, auf der die wichtigsten Grundlagen zum jeweiligen Thema zusammengestellt und mit zahlreichen Beispielsätzen veranschaulicht sind.

Dort können Sie Ihr Grammatikwissen aktivieren, bevor Sie mit den Übungen beginnen oder die eine oder andere Regel nachschlagen, mit der Sie beim Üben Probleme hatten.

So überprüfen Sie Ihren Lernfortschritt

Anhand der **Lösungen** ab Seite 121 können Sie Ihren Lernfortschritt überprüfen. Übungen, in denen Sie noch nicht ganz fehlerfrei waren, wiederholen Sie einfach nach einiger Zeit.

Setzen Sie vorne im **Inhaltsverzeichnis** einen Haken hinter alle Themen, die Sie erledigt haben. So können Sie auf einen Blick sehen, wie viel Sie schon trainiert haben.

Unbekannte Wörter? Kein Problem!

Alle schwierigen Wörter und Wendungen aus den Übungen können Sie in der englisch-deutschen Wortliste ab Seite 132 nachschlagen.

Viel Erfolg!

Ihre PONS Redaktion

INHALT

Checkliste Seite

TEIL 1: VERBFORMEN ÜBEN

TEIL 2: VERBEN RICHTIG BENUTZEN

1 VOLL- UND HILFSVERBEN

VOLLVERBEN

Vollverben haben eine lexikalische Bedeutung und bilden alleine oder mit Hilfsverben das Prädikat eines Satzes.

Janice reads a lot.	*Janice liest viel.*
Tom and Mia don't talk much.	*Tom und Mia reden nicht viel.*
Did you speak to Mia?	*Hast du mit Mia gesprochen?*

Vollverben können außerdem regelmäßig oder unregelmäßig sein.

» Kapitel 3: Regelmäßige und unregelmäßige Verben

Vorsicht bei Fragen: Ist ein Fragewort das Subjekt eines Fragesatzes, entspricht die Satzstellung dem Aussagesatz. Ist das Fragewort ein Objekt des Satzes, steht danach ein Hilfsverb und dann das Subjekt.

Who discovered America?	*Wer entdeckte Amerika?*
Who **does Tara** meet today?	*Wen trifft Tara heute?*

HILFSVERBEN

Die Verben **be, do, have** und **will** unterstützen die Vollverben bei der Bildung von Zeitformen, Fragen und Passiv.

» Verbtabellen Plus Englisch S. 36, 76, 102

Did you hear the news?	*Hast du die Neuigkeiten gehört?*
He has won the race.	*Er hat das Rennen gewonnen.*
They are running to the bus stop.	*Sie rennen gerade zur Bushaltestelle.*
You won't tell her, will you?	*Du wirst es ihr nicht verraten, oder?*

Die Hilfsverben **do, have** und **be** können auch als Vollverb auftreten.

I am doing my homework.	*Ich mache gerade meine Hausaufgaben.*
John has black hair.	*John hat schwarzes Haar.*
Her grandmother is very ill.	*Ihre Großmutter ist sehr krank.*

Tritt **be als Vollverb** auf, steht es in Fragen und Verneinungen ohne **do**.

Is the newspaper in the living-room?	*Ist die Zeitung im Wohnzimmer?*
The kids aren't hungry.	*Die Kinder sind nicht hungrig.*

★ **1.** Vervollständigen Sie diese Sätze, indem Sie die richtige Verbform im **present simple** auswählen.

a) Mr Harris **teach/teachs/teaches** geography at the local school.

b) Who here **knowes/know/knows** the rules of tennis?

c) **Are/Is/Be** you in a football team?

d) **Dos/Does/Do** you know the answer?

e) I **dont/don't/doesn't** do the ironing.

f) She **have/has/haes** a new computer.

» Kapitel 12: Present simple und progressive S. 55

★ **2.** Welche der hinterlegten Verben aus Übung 1 sind Vollverben?

teaches, knows, are, has, ______

★ **3.** Lesen Sie diese Sätze über eine Klassenfahrt und setzen Sie die Verben in die entsprechende Form des **past simple**.

a) We ______ (say) goodbye to our parents in front of the school.

b) After eight hours in the coach, we ______ (arrive) in the UK.

c) Our teacher ______ (take) us to the hotel.

d) In London, we ______ (see) lots of interesting sights and also ______ (go) to the theatre one evening.

e) We ______ (not meet) the Queen, though!

f) ______ (we/enjoy) it? Of course!

» Kapitel 14: Past tense und past perfect S. 63

★ **4.** Wie lauten die **past simple**-Formen dieser verneinten Verben?

a) isn't wasn't **b)** aren't weren't **c)** doesn't work didn't

d) hasn't hadn't **e)** don't do didn't

★ **5.** Ergänzen Sie die Lücken mit der passenden bejahten oder verneinten Verbform. Denken Sie daran, was bei **he/she/it** immer mit muss!

	to be (verneint)	**to do** (bejaht)	**to have** (bejaht)
I	am not	do	have
you	aren't	do	have
he/she/it	isn't	does	has
we	aren't	do	have
you	aren't	do	have
they	aren't	do	have

★ **6.** Auf die Fragen unten gibt es jeweils nur eine korrekt formulierte Antwort. Kreuzen Sie sie an.

a) Where is the bus stop?

☐ **A** I doesn't know.

☐ **B** I dont know.

☒ **C** I don't know.

b) Does he like football?

☐ **A** No, he dont.

☒ **B** No, he doesn't.

☐ **C** No, he doesnt.

c) Has she got a car?

☐ **A** Yes, she does.

☒ **B** Yes, she has.

d) Are they having fun?

☒ **A** Yes, they are.

☐ **B** Yes, they have.

★ **7.** Unterstreichen Sie in den folgenden Sätzen die Hilfsverben.

a) What do you know?

b) Who would like some tea?

c) Do you have bretzels, too?

d) How do you do?

e) Where have you been?

f) Why aren't they staying?

g) Have you seen this film?

h) Is it cold outside?

★★ **8.** Welche der nun in der vorigen Übung markierten Hilfsverben können auch als Vollverben verwendet werden?

____

★★ **9.** Zu den Fragen unten gibt es jeweils ein passendes **question tag**. Kreuzen Sie das richtige an.

a) It has been agreed on, ...

- ☐ A hadn't it?
- ☐ B wasn't it?
- ☒ C hasn't it?

b) But he went last year, ...

- ☒ A doesn't he?
- ☐ B didn't he?
- ☐ C wasn't he?

c) You did finish it though, ...

- ☒ A didn't you?
- ☐ B did you?
- ☐ C haven't you?

d) He hadn't been behaving oddly, ...

- ☐ A hadn't he?
- ☐ B was he?
- ☒ C had he?

e) She wasn't causing too much trouble, ...

- ☐ A wasn't she?
- ☐ B hadn't she?
- ☒ C was she?

★★ **10.** Unterstreichen Sie in den folgenden Sätzen jeweils das Vollverb und kreuzen Sie dann an, in welcher Zeitstufe die Sätze jeweils stehen.

	past	present	future
a) It is turning.	☐	☐	☐
b) You played.	☐	☐	☐
c) She will dream.	☐	☐	☐
d) I am going to go.	☐	☐	☐
e) They were going.	☐	☐	☐
f) I had had.	☐	☐	☐
g) They are going.	☐	☐	☐
h) It fell.	☐	☐	☐
i) I have got.	☐	☐	☐
j) He doesn't have.	☐	☐	☐

★★ **11.** Setzen Sie diese Verben ins **future perfect**. Benutzen Sie die Kurzformen.

a) I will go *I'll have gone*

b) You will not see ______________________

c) It will grow ______________________

d) She will forgive ______________________

e) They will not try ______________________

f) We will understand ______________________

g) He will not have ______________________

» Kapitel 11: Bildung future tenses S. 49

★★★ **12.** Formulieren Sie zu den folgenden Antworten die passenden Fragen. Fragen Sie nach dem unterstrichenen Wort und beginnen Sie mit **who** oder **what**.

a) Harold helps me. *Who helps me?*

b) Tina doesn't like cats. ______

c) Joe can call Andrew. ______

d) I am marrying Carter. ______

e) Andrew will see Mike. ______

f) Emma wants a new bike. ______

g) Mia would like some tea. ______

h) You know the secret. ______

★★★ **13.** Bringen Sie die Sätze wieder in die richtige Reihenfolge. Benutzen Sie die Kurzformen, wenn möglich.

a) has / help / not / she / trying / to / me / been / .

______

b) smoking / you / have /him / seen /?

______

c) moving / the / was / fast / catamaran / very / .

______

d) ill / had / they / been / really / looking / .

______

e) have / there / I / gone / would / not / .

______

2 MODALVERBEN

FUNKTION IM SATZ

Modalverben **(modal verbs)** sind Hilfsverben und werden nur zur Unterstützung eines Vollverbs benutzt.

Mit Modalverben wird die Bedeutung des Vollverbs im Satz näher bestimmt z. B. in Bezug darauf, wie zwingend oder mit welcher Sicherheit eine Handlung passiert, passieren wird oder passiert ist.

Zu den Modalverben gehören:

can **shall** **may** **will** **must** **could** **should** **might** **would** need

FORMEN

Modalverben haben in allen Personen die gleiche Form – sie haben also keine s-Form in der 3. Person Singular. Ihnen folgt immer ein Vollverb in der Grundform (Infinitiv), d. h. ohne **to**.

Nobody can predict the future.
I'm sure you will understand our situation.

Modalverben bilden Fragen, Kurzantworten, verneinte Aussagen und Frageanhängsel alleine, d. h. ohne das Hilfsverb **do**.

Can you play tennis?
I can go swimming, can't I? – Yes, you can!

ZEITEN UND ERSATZFORMEN

Modalverben werden grundsätzlich nur in der einfachen Gegenwart **(present simple)** verwendet. Für andere Zeiten benutzt man Ersatzformen wie **have to, be able to, be allowed to** usw.

We had to leave early.
He wasn't allowed to go to the cinema.
He will be able to repair his car.

» Kapitel 18: Gebrauch der Modalverben S. 88

★ **1.** Diese Buchstabenschlange besteht aus Modalverbformen im **present tense** und im **past tense**. Unterstreichen Sie nur die Formen im **present simple**!

couldmustmayshouldneedcanshallwould
mightwilloughtto

____

____

★ **2.** Vervollständigen Sie diese Sätze, indem Sie die richtige Modalverbform im **present simple** auswählen.

a) The children **must/musts/mustn't** be back home by seven.

b) **Need/Cans/Can** you help me for a moment?

c) He **must/need/needs** to be more careful in future.

d) I'm sorry, I **cant/can't/can** tell you the answer!

e) Tell him that he **must/musts/needs** finish it today.

f) You **need/neednt/needn't** carry my bag for me.

★★ **3.** Wie lauten die verneinten Formen der folgenden Modalverben bzw. Ersatzformen? Verwenden Sie Kurzformen, wenn möglich.

a) she will be able to ___won't___

b) he may ___may not___

c) they will be allowed to ___won't___

d) they must ___must not___

e) it would ___would not___

f) we had had to ___hadn't had to___

g) you ought to ___ought not___

★★ **4.** Verbinden Sie diese **modal verbs** mit ihren Vergangenheitsformen.

	●	A	wanted
a) can	●	B	have been able to
b) must	●	C	had to
c) should	●	D	was able to
d) want	●	E	have had to
	●	F	was supposed

★★ **5.** Ergänzen Sie die fehlenden Formen der **modal verbs**.

	conditional	**future**	**going to-future**
want			going to want
can	would be able to		
must		will have to	

★★★ **6.** Vervollständigen Sie diese Sätze mit der richtigen Form des Modalverbs im **conditional perfect**.

a) It's just what he ______________ (want).

b) If you hadn't been there, we ______________ (not can achieve) what we did.

c) If they had come, we ______________ (must find) a larger room.

d) I believe she ______________ (may do) anything she wanted.

e) What ______________ (you, do) if they had said no?

» Kapitel 8: Conditional S. 33

REGELMÄSSIGE, UNREGELMÄSSIGE UND REFLEXIVE VERBEN

3

REGELMÄSSIGE UND UNREGELMÄSSIGE VERBEN

» Übung 1–3, 5, 8–9

In der 3. Person Singular bildet man im **present simple** die Endung bei Verben
- wie **go** und **do** durch Anhängen von **-es**.
- mit der Endung Konsonant + **-y** durch Ersetzen von **-y** durch **-ies**.
- mit der Endung **-s** oder einem Zischlaut durch **-es**, gesprochen [ɪz].

go > goes kiss > kisses watch > watches
try > tries wish > wishes

» Kapitel 1: Voll- und Hilfsverben S. 6; Kapitel 4: Infinitiv, Partizipien und Gerund S. 20

Bei regelmäßigen Verben werden **past simple-** und **past participle**-Form durch Anhängen von **-ed** an die Grundform gebildet.

play > played

Endet die Grundform mit
- kurzem Vokal + Konsonant, wird der Konsonant verdoppelt.
- stummem **-e**, wird nur **-d** angehängt.
- Konsonant + **-y**, wird **-y** durch **-ied** ersetzt.

stop > stopped smile > smiled try > tried

Bei unregelmäßigen Verben muss man sowohl die **past simple-** als auch die **past participle**-Form auswendig lernen. Einige Beispiele sind:

catch, caught, caught drive, drove, driven read, read, read

REFLEXIVE VERBEN

» Übung 4, 6 und 7

Sind Subjekt und Objekt im Satz identisch, kann anstelle des Objekts ein Reflexivpronomen **(myself, yourself, ourselves...** – *mich, dich/Sie, uns... selbst)* stehen. Achtung: Vielen Verben, die im Deutschen reflexiv sind, entspricht im Englischen ein nicht-reflexives Verb!

You may help yourselves! Everything is on the table. – *Ihr könnt euch bedienen ...*
This is my cousin Lisa. Do you remember her? – ... *Erinnerst du dich an sie?*

Bei einer gegenseitigen Handlung verwendet man die reziproken Pronomen **each other/one another** – keine Reflexivpronomen!

Romeo and Juliet loved each other. – ... *sich (gegenseitig).*

★ **1.** Auf die Fragen unten gibt es jeweils nur eine korrekt formulierte Antwort. Kreuzen Sie sie an.

a) Which school does he go to?

☐ A He go to Fulchester Boys' School.

☐ B He goes to Fulchester Boys' School.

☐ C He gos to Fulchester Boys' School.

b) Can he play the piano?

☐ A No, but he tries hard!

☐ B No, but he trys hard!

☐ C No, but he try hard!

c) Does anyone here like football?

☐ A Ask Monica, she watchess it on TV.

☐ B Ask Monica, she watchs it on TV.

☐ C Ask Monica, she watches it on TV.

★ **2.** Ergänzen Sie die Lücken mit der passenden Verbform. Denken Sie daran, was bei he/she/it immer mit muss!

	to be	**to go**	**to see**
I	am		see
you		go	
he/she/it			
we		go	see
you	are		see
they		go	

» Kapitel 1: Voll- und Hilfsverben S. 6

★ **3.** Enden diese Verben im **present simple** in der 3. Person Singular **(he/she/it)** auf **-s** oder **-ies**? Schreiben Sie die entsprechende Form in die richtige Spalte.

say * buy * carry * try * cry * enjoy * study * play * hurry * pay

-s	**-ies**
______	______
______	______
______	______
______	______
______	______

» PONS Verbtabellen Plus Englisch S. 154, 48, 56, 84, 146, 144.

★★ **4.** Welches Pronomen passt hier? Manchmal muss die Lücke auch frei bleiben, da manche Verben im Deutschen reflexiv sind, im Englischen aber nicht.

a) Frieda was angry with **oneself/herself/himself/---**.

b) I kept telling **myself/me/---/ourselves** that everything was alright.

c) You should concentrate **you/myself/---/yourself**.

d) He often talks to **himself/herself/themselves/---**.

e) Let's meet **ourselves/us/yourself/---** tomorrow.

f) We really enjoyed **us/yourself/---/ourselves** in the mountains.

g) They admired **themselves/---/them/oneself** in the mirror.

h) The door closes **its/itself/---/oneself**.

i) I apologized **myself/me/---/you** to her.

j) She wonders **himself/her/herself/---** what's wrong with her car.

k) Elderly people often can't look after **oneself/---/themselves/them** any more.

★★ **5.** Welche dieser Verben stehen im **past simple**, welche sind Partizipien und welche können beides sein?

run * swung * risen * sawn * blew * paid * left * brought * lay * beat * stolen

past simple	**past simple/participle**	**participle**
______	______	______
______	______	______
______	______	______
______	______	______

★★ **6.** Im Deutschen sind einige Verben reflexiv, die im Englischen ohne Reflexivpronomen stehen. Jeweils welches Verb kann im Englischen reflexiv sein?

a) ☐ A argue ☐ B sit down ☐ C cut ☐ D be interested in

b) ☐ A behave ☐ B buy ☐ C complain about ☐ D get dressed

c) ☐ A imagine ☐ B remember ☐ C concentrate (on) ☐ D help

★★★ **7.** Setzen Sie entweder **each other** oder das fehlende Reflexivpronomen **(myself, yourself, himself, herself, ourselves, yourselves, themselves)** ein.

a) Trust in her. She can do it ______.

b) I look at ______ in the mirror.

c) Here's the tea. Please help ______.

d) Stop quarrelling and help ______.

e) Most of the guests didn't like the food, including ______.

f) We never go to school together because we hate ______.

g) We see ______ every day.

★★★ **8.** Tragen Sie das jeweilige Verb in der **past simple**-Form ein.

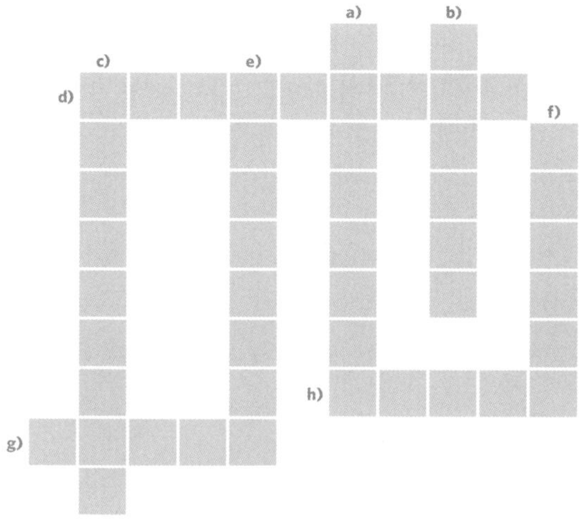

Down:
a) to backslide
b) to resend
c) to persuade
e) to undercut
f) to mislead

Across:
d) to populate
g) to reset
h) to dive

★★★ **9.** Verhalten sich die folgenden Verben im **past simple** regelmäßig oder unregelmäßig oder gibt es zwei Varianten? Schreiben Sie die **past simple**-Formen in die richtige Spalte.

reach • quit • strike • lean • tend • learn • bet • wear • fight • turn • spell • look

regular	regular/irregular	irregular
______	______	______
______	______	______
______	______	______
______	______	______

4 INFINITIV, PARTIZIPIEN UND GERUND

DER INFINITIV

Der Infinitiv (Grundform des Verbs) enthält keine Angaben zu Person und Zahl.
Julie wants to travel all over Australia. (Inf.) <> Julie travels a lot. (3. Person Sg.)

Der Infinitiv kann von allen Verben außer den modalen Hilfsverben gebildet werden. Er kann mit und ohne **to** auftreten:

Jane wants to help me.	Mike can help you, too.

Weitere Formen des Infinitivs sind z. B.:

verneinte Form: **not** + **to** ...	She promised not to ask him. *Sie versprach, ihn nicht zu fragen.*
Passivform: **(to) be** + **past participle**	My car had to be repaired. ... *musste repariert werden.*
progressive form: **(to) be** + **present participle**	Jenny called. She seems to be doing fine. ... *Es scheint ihr (momentan) gut zu gehen.*

» Kapitel 23: Gebrauch des Infinitivs S. 106

PARTIZIPIEN UND GERUND

Das **present participle** und das **gerund** haben die gleiche, von Person und Zahl unabhängige Form. Sie wird aus der Grundform des Verbs + **-ing** gebildet und daher auch **ing-**Form genannt.

Die einfache Passivform der **ing**-Form wird gebildet aus:

being + **past participle**	She was afraid of being sent abroad.

Das **past participle** wird bei regelmäßigen Verben durch Anhängen von **–ed** an die Grundform gebildet.

» Kapitel 3: Regelmäßige, unregelmäßige u. reflexive Verben S. 15

Weitere Formen sind die

(aktive) Perfektform: **having** + **past participle**	passive Perfektform: **having been** + **past participle**

» Kapitel 25: Gebrauch von Partizipien S. 116;
» Kapitel 24: Gebrauch des Gerund S. 112

★ **1.** In der Wortschlange verstecken sich Infinitive, **present participles** (**ing**-Formen) und **past participles**. Können Sie zehn korrekte Formen finden?

goeondoingweswulbewalkingtalkmakengadone
nsthavingsprkrainduydhaddydsb

Infinitive: ______________________

present participles: ______________________

past participles: ______________________

★ **2.** Bei einigen dieser Verben müssen Sie bei der Bildung des **present participle** (**ing**-Form) besonders auf die Schreibung achten. Notieren Sie diese **ing**-Formen.

leave * smile * put * look * play * write * see * run * lie * happen * be * go

______________________ ______________________

______________________ ______________________

______________________ ______________________

★★ **3.** Bilden Sie jeweils die fehlenden Formen des Verbs.

Infinitiv	present participle	past participle
	answering	
sit		
		loved
		cut
see		
die		
make		

★★ **4.** In diesen Buchstabensalaten stecken Partizipien. Schreiben Sie sie auf. Handelt es sich jeweils um ein **present participle** (PR) oder ein **past participle** (PA)?

a) odotunsred ______________________________ __________

b) signcussid ______________________________ __________

c) gintivin ______________________________ __________

d) gorfotent ______________________________ __________

★★ **5.** Je eins der vier **past participles** in der Reihe ist falsch. Kreuzen Sie es an.

a) ☐ A beated ☐ B eaten ☐ C given ☐ D created

b) ☐ A sung ☐ B sut ☐ C swum ☐ D drunk

c) ☐ A driven ☐ B taught ☐ C caught ☐ D sayed

★★★ **6.** Setzen Sie ein **present participle** bzw. eine **ing**-Form oder ein **past participle** der vorgegebenen Verben ein, um die Lücken korrekt zu ergänzen.

Hey Jane, how are you **(a)** ______________ (do)? Have you **(b)** ______________ (find) a summer job yet? **(c)** ______________ (confine) to my room because of all that **(d)** ______________ (revise) for my exams, I haven't **(e)** ______________ (have) time to look for one. You told me your brother will **(f)** ______________ (work) at the ice-cream parlour again. **(g)** ______________ (eat) and **(h)** ______________ (enjoy) an ice cream there myself, I am very jealous of him!

Best, Patrick

LEICHT VERWECHSELBARE VERBEN

Einige englische Verben haben ähnliche oder sogar gleiche Grundformen, die sehr leicht verwechselt werden können.

Julie lies in bed.	*Julie liegt im Bett.*
Tom often lies.	*Tom lügt oft.*

Auch bei Vergangenheitsformen solcher Verben besteht aufgrund der ähnlichen Schreibweise Verwechslungsgefahr. Vergleichen Sie:

lie, lay, lain down	▪ *sich hinlegen* (um auszuruhen oder zu schlafen)
lie, lied, lied	▪ *lügen*
lay, laid, laid (s.b./s.th.) down	▪ *jdn./etwas flach hinlegen*

I didn't feel quite well so I lay down for a bit.	*... legte ich mich ein wenig hin.*
I think Tom lied to me.	*Ich glaube, Tom hat mich belogen.*
She laid the injured cat down on a blanket.	*Sie legte die verletzte Katze auf eine Decke.*

Weitere Beispiele sind:

see, saw, seen – *sehen*	< >	saw, sawed, sawed – *sägen*
strike, struck, struck – *schlagen*	< >	stroke, stroked, stroked – *streicheln*
find, found, found – *finden*	< >	found, founded, founded – *gründen*

» Kapitel 3: Regelmäßige, unregelmäßige und reflexive Verben S. 15

Außerdem gibt es englische Verben, die sich nur in der Aussprache bzw. Betonung von anderen Wörtern unterscheiden. Sie heißen Homographe.

Einsilbige Homographe sind z. B.:	Zweisilbige Homographe sind z. B.
close [kləʊs] – *nah*	present ['prezənt] – *Geschenk*
close [kləʊz] – *schließen*	present [prɪ'zent] – *schenken*
read [riːd] – *lesen*	import ['ɪmpɔːt] – *Importware*
read [red] – *las, gelesen*	import [ɪm'pɔːt] – *importieren*

Homophone sind Wörter, die gleich klingen, sich aber in Bedeutung und Schreibung unterscheiden, z. B.:

brake – *bremsen; Bremse*	< [breɪk] >	*break – zerbrechen; Pause*
sea – *Meer*	< [siː] >	*see – sehen*
knew – *wusste*	< [njuː] >	*new – neu*

» Kapitel 20: Leicht verwechselbare Verben und Wendungen S. 94

★ **1.** Wählen Sie die richtige Verbform im **present simple** aus.

a) The sun **rises/raises** in the east.

b) Where's Tommy? I can't **see/saw** him anywhere.

c) Pam says you can **found/find** beautiful things on a beach.

d) If you don't feel good, **lay/lie** down for a moment!

e) Mia, please be careful with that vase! Don't **break/brake** it!

f) Dad always unfolds the newspaper and **lies/lays** it flat on the table to read.

★★ **2.** Welche dieser ähnlichen Verbformen sind zugleich **present simple-Form** als auch **past simple-Form** (jeweils für verschiedene Verben)?

roselaidseeliedsawstrikelayraisedfoundlierise
struckawedstrokefounded

★★ **3.** Füllen Sie die Lücken mit den passenden Verbformen aus dem Kasten. Füllen Sie dann die Leerzeilen mit den „übrigen" Formen.

found (2x) * founded (2x) * raise * rise * rose * raised (2x) * saw * sawn * seen * see * find

Infinitiv	**past simple**	**past participle**
	found	
		risen
	saw	
	sawed	

★★ **4.** Für die folgenden Fragen sehen Sie mehrere Antworten. Alle sind grammatisch korrekt, aber nur eine passt jeweils sinnvoll zur Frage. Welche?

a) What did Mary say?

- ☐ A She lay on the sofa.
- ☐ B She lied about the sofa.
- ☐ C She laid a blanket on the sofa.

b) The dog looks relaxed. What did you do with him?

- ☐ A I stroked him a lot.
- ☐ B I struck him a lot.

» PONS Verbtabellen Plus Englisch S. 122-23.

★★★ **5.** Sie schreiben Ihrem Freund in Kanada eine E-Mail. Füllen Sie die Lücken.

Hey Joe, did you by any chance ______________ (finden) **(a)** that photo I liked so much? You know, the one that I took with your old-fashioned camera when we were camping, the sun had just ______________ (aufgehen) **(b)** and you were ______________ (sägen) **(c)** that tree which had been ______________ (treffen) **(d)** by lightning into firewood. I think I last ______________ (sehen) **(e)** the photo at your place on my last evening. You drove me to the airport and as soon as the plane had taken off I ______________ (zurücklehnen) **(f)** and tried to sleep. Now I can't remember if I packed it. Please tell me if you've ______________ (finden) **(g)** it by any chance. – Thanks again for looking.

Best, Patrick

★★★ **6.** Manche Verben unterscheiden sich nur durch ihre Aussprache von anderen Wörtern. Ordnen Sie den Wörtern unten die richtige Aussprache zu.

A [wɪnd] B [waʊnd] C [raʊ] D [rəʊ] E [wuːnd] F [waɪnd]

a) row *(Reihe; rudern)*

b) row *(Streit; sich streiten)*

c) wind *(Wind; Kurve)*

d) wind *(aufziehen, z. B. eine Uhr)*

e) wound *(Vergangenh. v. d) wind)*

f) wound *(Wunde; verwunden)*

6 IMPERATIV

Um Aufforderungssätze zu bilden, benötigt man die Imperativform des Verbs. Sie entspricht der Infinitivform und ist im Singular und Plural gleich.

Come in.	*Komm/Kommt/Kommen Sie herein!*
Have a cup of coffee.	*Trink/Trinkt/Trinken Sie eine Tasse Kaffee.*

Verneinte Aufforderungssätze werden mit don't + Infinitiv gebildet (förmlich auch: **do not** + Infinitiv).

Die Aufforderung wirkt grundsätzlich höflicher, wenn **please** voran- oder nachgestellt wird.

Verneinte Aufforderungen mit **ever** drücken eine Ermahnung aus. Anstatt mit ... **not** + **ever** kann die Ermahnung auch mit dem Wort **never** beginnen.

Don't tell Mum.	*Sag's/Sagt's/Sagen Sie es nicht Mama!*
Please do not smoke in these rooms.	*Bitte in diesen Räumen nicht rauchen.*
Don't ever forget ... Never forget ...	*Vergiss/Vergesst/Vergessen Sie niemals ...!*

... your umbrella when you're in Scotland.

Bezieht sich der Sprechende selbst in die Aufforderung mit ein, wird die Formulierung **let's** + Infinitiv bzw. **let's not** + Infinitiv verwendet. Die Vollform **let us** + Infinitiv wird nur im förmlichen Stil verwendet.

Let's go to Angelo's and have a pizza there.	*Gehen wir ...*
Oh no, let's not go out tonight. I've got a headache.	*... gehen wir lieber nicht ...*
Let us pray.	*Lasset uns beten.*

Um einer Aufforderung noch mehr Druck zu verleihen, kann man ein zusätzliches **you** einfügen:

You be careful.	*Sei/Seid/Seien Sie bloß vorsichtig!*
Don't you try this again.	*Versuch/Versucht/Versuchen Sie das nicht noch einmal!*

Ein zusätzliches **do** kann man verwenden, wenn man nachdrücklich um etwas bitten will:

Do be punctual.	*Sei/Seid/Seien Sie unbedingt pünktlich!*
Do come in.	*Komm/Kommt/Kommen Sie doch bitte herein!*

» Kapitel 19: Gebrauch des Imperativs S. 92

★ **1.** Vervollständigen Sie die Imperativsätze unten mit der richtigen Verbform.

a) Jim, **turn off/turns off/turned off** the radio, please!

b) Mia and Kate, please **stops/stopping/stop** running!

c) **Don't drives/Don't drive/Doesn't drive** so fast! It's raining.

d) **Mind/Minded/Minds** the step.

e) **Am/Be/Are** careful, you two.

★★ **2.** Diese Imperativsätze sind durcheinander geraten. Wie lauten sie richtig?

a) this/ at/ try/ to do/ home/ don't/.

____

b) have/ here/ let's/ picnic/ our/.

____

c) forget /your/ to lock/ door/ never/.

____

★★★ **3.** Können Sie die folgenden Sätze als Imperative formulieren?
Achtung, es können bejahte und verneinte Imperative vorkommen.

a) Would you like to go to the cinema?

____

b) I don't think we should visit Aunt Mary today.

____

c) Why don't we go swimming instead?

____

7 PASSIV

Im Passiv werden alle Zeitformen aus einer Form von **be** und dem **past participle** gebildet.

» Kapitel 4: Infinitiv, Partizipien und Gerund S. 20

The dustbins are emptied every Wednesday.	*Die Mülleimer werden … geleert.*
Were they emptied last week?	*Wurden sie letzte Woche geleert?*
They haven't been emptied yet.	*Sie sind noch nicht geleert worden.*
The lawn will be mowed next week.	*Der Rasen wird nächste Woche gemäht werden.*

Die progressive-Form erscheint im Passiv meist nur im **present** und **past tense**:

am/are/is being + past participle	The window is being replaced right now.
was/were being + past participle	The dustbins were being emptied and the children were watching.

Das Passiv mit Modalverben wird für Aussagen mit Gegenwartsbezug mit dem Infinitiv von **be + past participle** gebildet, für Aussagen mit Vergangenheitsbezug mit **have been + past participle**.

It must be mowed earlier.	*Er muss früher gemäht werden.*
The window should have been repaired weeks ago.	*Das Fenster hätte vor Wochen repariert werden sollen.*

Viele Aktivsätze mit direktem Objekt lassen sich in Passivsätze umformen. Das ursprüngliche Objekt wird dabei zum Subjekt des Passivsatzes. Der Verursacher der Handlung wird oft nicht genannt, kann aber als **by-agent** auftreten. Gehört zum Verb eine Präposition, steht diese auch im Passivsatz beim Verb.

Aktiv:	Dad mows the lawn.	Somebody broke into our friends' house.
Passiv:	The lawn is mowed (by Dad).	Our friends' house was broken into.

Einige englische Verben (**give**, **send**, **show**, etc.) können zwei Objekte haben. Dann gibt es zwei Möglichkeiten, Passivsätze zu bilden.

Aktiv:	I sent Mum a birthday card.
Passiv:	Mum was sent a birthday card.
Passiv:	A birthday card was sent to Mum.

Umgangssprachlich wird anstatt des Passivs manchmal das **get**-Passiv verwendet. Man bildet es aus **get + past participle**.

Our cat got bitten by the neighbour's mouse.	*Unsere Katze wurde … gebissen.*

» Kapitel 22: Gebrauch des Passivs S. 102

★ **1.** **Welche der Sätze sind aktiv? Welche passiv? Ordnen Sie richtig zu.**

a) The dogs were outside.

b) Laura went for a walk.

c) The decision is made.

d) All the apples were eaten.

e) My dad is angry with me.

f) The animals are killed.

g) I wasn't sure about it.

h) I was beaten in the game.

Aktiv: ______________________________

Passiv: ______________________________

★ **2.** **In den folgenden passiven Sätzen wird die handelnde Person mit by angeschlossen. Ordnen Sie die Sätze den passenden Bildern zu.**

A

B

C

D

a) The children are helped by a friendly teacher. ___

b) The call is taken by the receptionist. ___

c) The fire was extinguished by firefighters. ___

d) The car was repaired by a mechanic. ___

★ **3.** **Unterstreichen Sie die zwischen den Formen versteckte Aktivform.**

a) had done ⋆ is done ⋆ was done ⋆ has been done ⋆ are done

b) were seen ⋆ is seen ⋆ am seen ⋆ are seen ⋆ have seen

c) was going ⋆ was seen ⋆ was done ⋆ was kept

★★ **4.** Wie lauten die **progressive**-Formen der folgenden passiven Verbformen?

a) It is repaired ______

b) The shirts are made ______

c) We were helped ______

d) I am examined ______

e) My bike was stolen ______

★★ **5.** Wandeln Sie folgende Sätze ins **get**-Passiv um.

a) He was badly hurt in the accident.

______

b) Your bike might be stolen outside.

______

c) Unfortunately we were bitten by mosquitoes at the picnic.

______

★★ **6.** Sind diese Verbformen Aktiv- oder Passivformen? Schreiben Sie A (Aktiv) bzw. P (Passiv) dahinter. Wandeln Sie sie dann in die jeweils andere Form um.

a) I have been offered ___

b) It was losing ___

c) They have been looking after ___

d) They were told ___

e) She had offended ___

f) We are leaving ___

g) I was being beaten ___

h) She had been given ___

a) *I have offered*

b) ______

c) ______

d) ______

e) ______

f) ______

g) ______

h) ______

★★ **7.** Bringen Sie diese Passivsätze im **present** und **past tense** in die richtige Reihenfolge. Achten Sie dabei auf **progressive**-Formen.

a) to / letters / president / written / are / Many / the /.

____

b) by / right now / is / Our / firemen / rescued / cat / neighbour's / being /.

____

c) criticized / Politicians / for / abstract / using / language / are /.

____

d) were / the / children / The / by / cupcakes / eaten /.

____

e) the / was / yesterday / car / taken / to / My / garage /.

____

f) repaired / car / being / While / was / my /, I went by train.

____

★★ **8.** Formen Sie nun die jeweils unten angegebenen Sätze aus Aufgabe 7 in eine Frage und/oder eine Verneinung um.

a) Frage: ______________________________

b) Frage: ______________________________

c) Verneinung: ______________________________

d) Frage: ______________________________

e) Verneinung: ______________________________

f) Verneinung: ______________________________

★★ **9.** Vervollständigen Sie diese Sätze mit der korrekten Passivform des Verbs.

a) After six weeks, the dog ______________ (give, past simple) to new owners.

b) He ______________ (already/award, past perfect) several prizes for his outstanding performance.

c) His last album ______________ (finally/release, present perfect) after all these years.

d) The play ______________ (perform, going to-future) at the end of the school year.

e) The news ______________ (make, will-future) public until the government gives its permission.

f) The school cafeteria ______________ (refit, present progr) this term.

g) Dogs ______________ (must/keep, present tense) on a leash.

h) The rear light of my car ______________ (should/replace, present perfect) have been replaced when it was checked last week.

★★★ **10.** Wandeln Sie die Aktivsätze in Passivsätze um, ohne die handelnde Person in den Passivsätzen zu nennen (kein **by-agent**). Behalten Sie die Zeit bei.

a) They win the match. ______________

b) He discovered the small island. ______________

c) She throws the ball. ______________

d) They catch the thief. ______________

e) They washed our clothes. ______________

f) I made a mistake. ______________

g) He is counting the eggs. ______________

CONDITIONAL UND CONDITIONAL PERFECT

8

Das **conditional** wird für alle Personen wie folgt gebildet:

bejaht bzw. verneint:	**would/'d** bzw. **would not/wouldn't**	+ **Infinitiv**
mit Modalverb:	**could/should/might**	+ **Infinitiv**

I'm sure Julia would help me.	*Ich bin sicher, Julia würde mir helfen.*
Chris wouldn't be happy.	*Chris wäre nicht glücklich. (ugs.: ...würde nicht glücklich sein.)*
I could ask Julia to help me.	*Ich könnte Julia bitten, mir zu helfen.*

Ins Deutsche wird das **conditional** korrekt mit einer Form des Konjunktivs II oder mit *würde(-st/-t/-n) + Infinitiv* übersetzt. Die Modalverbformen **could**, **should** und **might** sind auch **conditional**-Formen und werden wie **would** verwendet.

Die Ersatzformen für Modalverbformen lauten im **conditional**:

would/'d	+ **be able to** (für **can**, **could**)
bzw.	+ **be going to** (für **will**, **shall**)
would not/wouldn't	+ **be allowed to** (für **may**, **might**, verneint für **mustn't**)
	+ **be supposed to** (für **should**, **ought to**)
	+ **have to** (bejaht für **must**, verneint für **needn't**)

I would have to go if necessary.	*Ich müsste notfalls hingehen.*
She would have had to call a taxi.	*Sie hätte ein Taxi rufen müssen.*

Das **conditional perfect** wird für alle Personen wie folgt gebildet:

bejaht bzw. verneint:	**would/'d**	
	would not/wouldn't	+ **have** + **past participle**
mit Modalverb:	**must/could** etc.	
mit Ersatzform:	**would** + **have** + **past participle d. Ersatzform** + **Infinitiv**	

Jo would have got sick.	*Jo wäre krank geworden.*
Would you have told me the truth?	*Hättest du mir die Wahrheit gesagt?*
I wouldn't have paid that.	*Das hätte ich nicht bezahlt.*
She may have missed the bus.	*Sie könnte den Bus verpasst haben.*

Ins Deutsche wird das **conditional perfect** korrekt mit einer Form des Konjunktivs II Perfekt übersetzt.

» Kapitel 16: Gebrauch des Conditional S. 77;
» Kapitel 18: Gebrauch der Modalverben S. 88

★ **1.** Eine der Antworten passt nicht zu der jeweiligen Frage. Kreuzen Sie die drei an, die passen.

a) What would you do with the money?

- ☐ **A** I would have spent it all at once.
- ☐ **B** I would donate it to charity.
- ☐ **C** I would put it in the bank.
- ☐ **D** I would buy a huge house.

b) What would she have done if she had known?

- ☐ **A** She would have gone straight over there!
- ☐ **B** She wouldn't have gone to the party, that's for sure.
- ☐ **C** She wouldn't have given him her number.
- ☐ **D** She would be very upset by it.

★ **2.** Schreiben Sie diese verneinten Verben ins **conditional** um. Benutzen Sie dabei die gängigen Kurzformen.

a) It isn't ____________________

b) They don't watch ____________________

c) We don't ____________________

d) You don't go ____________________

e) They can't ____________________

f) You don't know ____________________

g) She hasn't ____________________

h) I don't want ____________________

★ **3.** Setzen Sie die fehlenden Apostrophen und zeichnen Sie die Leerzeichen mit einem senkrechten Strich ein, so dass die **conditional**-Formen korrekt sind.

a) shewouldntleave

b) Iwouldnthavethought

c) itwouldntdo

d) theywouldbeseeing

e) hedhavehad

f) youdbehaving

★ **4.** Welche dieser Sätze stehen im **conditional perfect simple**? Kreuzen Sie sie an. Achtung Verwechslungsgefahr: **Would** und **had** haben die gleiche Kurzform.

- ☐ **A** Would you have told me the truth?
- ☐ **B** I'd paid for the tickets.
- ☐ **C** I'd have apologized for that.
- ☐ **D** I'd pay for the tickets.
- ☐ **E** I'd have paid for the tickets.
- ☐ **F** Wouldn't Edward have agreed?
- ☐ **G** I'd apologized for that.
- ☐ **H** I would have spoken to my wife at first.

★★ **5.** Übertragen Sie die folgenden **conditional**-Sätze ins Deutsche.

a) You could ask Granny. She would know what to do.

____

b) I'm still wondering whether I should have bought these tickets.

____

★★ **6.** Diese **conditional**-Sätze sind durcheinander geraten. Bringen Sie die Wörter wieder in die richtige Reihenfolge.

a) have / I / apologized / would / provoking / for / her /.

____

b) he / message / wouldn't / Why / leave / a /?

____

c) should / You / the / to / have / boss / first / spoken /.

____

d) the / sure / tell / they / I'm / would / truth / me /.

____

★★★ **7.** Tragen Sie die fehlenden Formen der Modalverben in die Tabelle ein.

	must	**can**	**may**	**should, ought to**
conditional	would have to			
conditional perfect	would have had to			

★★★ **8.** Bei diesen Fragen fehlt das abschließende **question tag**. Ergänzen Sie es.

a) He couldn't have forgotten about it, ______________?

b) She wouldn't have forgotten about it, ______________?

c) I shouldn't have opened it, ______________?

d) However, you would have had to do it, ______________?

e) They would never betray each other, ______________?

BILDUNG: PRESENT TENSE UND PRESENT PERFECT

9

PRESENT SIMPLE UND PROGRESSIVE

» Übung 1-8

Das **present simple** entspricht bei den Personen **I, you, we, you, they** dem Infinitiv des Verbs. Bei den Personen **he, she, it** (3. Person Singular) wird ein **-s** an den Infinitiv angehängt (» Kapitel 3: Regelmäßige, unregelmäßige u. reflexive Verben S. 15). Zur Bildung von verneinten Aussagesätzen und Fragen sowie Kurzantworten benötigt man das Hilfsverb **do** (oder ein modales Hilfsverb).

» Kapitel 12: Present simple und progressive S. 55

I/You/We/You/They	play tennis.	I/You/We/You/They	don't play.
He/She/It	plays tennis.	He/She/It	doesn't play.

Does he/she/it play? — Yes, he/she/it does./ No, he/she/it doesn't.
Can you play? — Yes, I can./ No, I can't.

Das **present progressive** wird gebildet aus **am/are/is** + **present participle** (=-**ing**-Form » Kapitel 4: Infinitiv, Partizipien und Gerund S. 20).

I am/I'm He/She/It is /'s You/We/You/They are/'re	} playing.	I'm not He/She/It's not/isn't You/We/You/They're not/aren't	} playing.
Am I/ Is he (she, it)/ Are you (we, you, they)	} playing?	Yes, I am./ he (...) is./ you (...) are. No, I'm not./ he (...) 's not./ you (...) 're not.	

PRESENT PERFECT SIMPLE UND PROGRESSIVE

» Übung 9-15

Das **present perfect** simple wird gebildet aus **has/have** + **past participle** (=Infinitiv + **-ed** oder unregelmäßige Verbform » Kapitel 4: Infinitiv, Partizipien u. Gerund S. 20). » Kapitel 13: Present perfect simple und progressive S. 59

I/You/We/You/They	have (not bzw. -n't)/'ve (not)	} finished.
He/She/It	has (not bzw. -n't)/'s (not)	

Have(n't) I (...) finished? — Has(n't) he (...) finished?
Yes/No, I (...) have/haven't. — Yes/No, he (...) has/hasn't.

Das **present perfect progressive** wird gebildet aus **has/have** + **been** + **present participle** (= **-ing**-Form » Kapitel 4: Infinitiv, Partizipien und Gerund S. 20).

I/You/We/You/They	have (not bzw. -n't) been	} diving.
He/She/It	has (not bzw. -n't) been	

Have(n't) I (...) been diving? — Has(n't) he (...) been diving?
Yes/No, I (...) have/haven't. — Yes/No, he (...) has/hasn't.

Present Tense

★ **1.** Diese Buchstabenschlange besteht aus Verben im **present simple**. Können Sie sie alle finden?

writeeatsshowseeslikesgodoesamsleep
isfliesareteaches

____

____

★ **2.** Welche der Verben in der Box erscheinen normalerweise nur im **present simple**? Schreiben Sie sie auf.

hope * become * see * carry * know * eat * taste * read * belong * laugh * sound * work
hate * grow * forget * love * drink * imagine * wear * cost * get * understand

____________	____________	____________
____________	____________	____________
____________	____________	____________
____________	____________	____________

★ **3.** Setzen Sie die Verben in die entsprechende Form des **present simple**.

a) School in England usually ____________ (begin) at about 8.30am.

b) There ____________ (be) often an assembly before lessons start.

c) Each class ____________ (have) a form teacher who they ____________ (see) every day.

d) The bell ____________ (ring) at the end of each period. Period ____________ (be) another word for lesson.

e) The school day mostly ____________ (end) at around 3.00pm or 4.00pm.

★ **4.** Kreuzen Sie jeweils die korrekte Antwort im **present progressive** an.

a) Where are your family going on holiday?

☐ **A** They are going to Cyprus for two weeks.

☐ **B** They is going to Cyprus for two weeks.

☐ **C** They are go to Cyprus for two weeks.

b) I'm going out. Who else is coming?

☐ **A** We come!

☐ **B** We are!

☐ **C** We coming!

c) Is anyone here not having fun?

☐ **A** I not.

☐ **B** I'm not.

☐ **C** I not having fun.

d) What is she doing in there?

☐ **A** She is put on her make-up.

☐ **B** She putting on her make-up.

☐ **C** She is putting on her make-up.

e) What are you writing about?

☐ **A** We are write about polo.

☐ **B** We are writing about polo.

☐ **C** We is writing about polo.

★★ **5.** Ergänzen Sie die fehlenden Bestätigungsfragen **(question tags)**.

a) You don't want to play outside, ____________________?

b) Robbie and Ken are eating apples, ____________________?

c) Bob and Carl cook together quite often, ____________________?

d) It isn't raining at the moment, ____________________?

e) Cindy can't take the call, ____________________?

f) We must hurry, ____________________?

g) The moon goes round the earth, ____________________?

h) The plane's on time, ____________________?

★★ **6.** Füllen Sie die Lücken mit der passenden Verbform.

Infinitiv	present simple (3. Ps. Sing.) bejaht/verneint	present progressive (3. Ps. Sg.) bejaht/verneint
do		
		is being/
try		
	/doesn't take	

★★★ **7.** Bilden Sie aus den Vorgaben Fragen im **present progressive**.

a) enjoy / the Millers / their / through Canada / trip /?

____

b) tonight / go / where / you /?

____

c) a car race / on TV / again / Dad / watch /?

____

★★★ **8.** Ihre Großmutter ist zu Besuch. Sie muss im Gespräch öfter nachfragen. Ergänzen Sie ihre Fragen im **present simple** bzw. **progressive**!

a) I like your home-made cookies! – What ______________________?

b) I am just speaking to Matt on the phone. – ______________________ to Matt?

c) Mom is looking for her shoes. – What ______________________ for?

d) The Millers say they are going on holiday tomorrow. –

Who ______________________ on holiday tomorrow?

e) Their plane leaves at 6.30. – When ______________________?

Present Perfect

★ **9.** Schreiben Sie diese Verben im **present perfect simple** in die verneinte Form um. Achten Sie auf die Kurzformen, die sich dabei ergeben.

a) I've gone ____________________ **b)** She's been ____________________

c) We've seen ____________________ **d)** He's done ____________________

e) They've eaten ____________________ **f)** It's taken ____________________

★ **10.** Vervollständigen Sie diese Sätze, indem Sie die richtige Verbform im **present perfect simple** auswählen.

a) The hot cup has ____________ **leave/left** a stain on the couch.

b) Christine has ____________ **go/been** to New York twice already.

c) Have you ____________ **hear/heard** about Rajesh and Nicky?

d) What ____________ **has/did** she done about it, then?

e) If you have ____________ **finish/finished**, then you can sit quietly.

f) ____________ **Did/Have** they really eaten all of the cake already?

★ **11.** Schreiben Sie diese Verben in die verneinte Form des **present perfect progressive** um und benutzen Sie die Kurzformen, die sich ergeben.

a) I'm going ____________________

b) They're making ____________________

c) She's leaving ____________________

d) We're choosing ____________________

e) He's informing ____________________

f) It's developing ____________________

★ **12.** Setzen Sie die Verben in die korrekte Form des **present perfect progressive**.

a) The internet ________________ (change) our society for over twenty years now.

b) Social networking sites ________________ (grow) fast since 2005.

c) Older kinds of media like newspapers and television ________________ (struggle) to keep up with recent changes.

d) Internet search engines ________________ (expand) their capacity non-stop over the last decade.

e) Some academics at top universities ________________ (study) the effects of new technology, but do not have clear results yet.

f) Young people across the world ________________ (use) the internet to exchange ideas and learn more about each other.

★★ **13.** Bilden Sie aus den vorgegebenen Bruchstücken Sätze im **present perfect simple**. Achten Sie darauf, ob der Satz als Frage formuliert werden soll.

a) David / leave / the money / in an envelope?

____

b) I / forget / pass on / the message.

____

c) their teacher / not ask for / the homework / yet.

____

d) you / write / an exciting story.

____

e) she / see / the film / already?

____

★★ **14.** Vervollständigen Sie die Sätze mit den korrekten **question tags**. Achtung, es sind Sätze im **present perfect simple** und **progressive** dabei!

a) Claudia has been spending hours in the bathroom, ____________________?

b) Richard hasn't been watching TV for hours, ____________________?

c) They've been playing football again, ____________________?

d) He's won several tournaments this year, ____________________?

e) You're still in your pyjamas! You haven't been lazy all this time, ____________________?

f) I've repaired your computer, ____________________?

g) We haven't seen each other for quite a long time, ____________________?

★★ **15.** Ergänzen Sie die fehlenden Verbteile in diesen Sätzen im **present perfect simple** bzw. **progressive.** Es handelt sich immer um Formen von **be** oder **have.**

a) I've ____________________ a bit lazy so far this year.

b) David tells me he has been ____________________ piano lessons.

c) They have ____________________ doing their homework all afternoon.

d) Has she ____________________ having a good time since she went to Australia?

e) He ____________________ done nothing to keep his promise so far.

f) What ____________________ you been doing all afternoon? We've just ____________________ a great time in the park.

g) ____________________ a break. You ____________________ been working without a break for over three hours.

h) Haven't we met before? It must ____________________ been just recently.

i) I've ____________________ sick all night. I shouldn't ____________________ eaten that fish.

10 BILDUNG: PAST TENSE UND PAST PERFECT

PAST SIMPLE UND PROGRESSIVE » Übung 1–7

Die **past simple**-Form lautet für alle Personen **Infinitiv** + **-ed** (oder unregelmäßige Verbform). Fragen bildet man mit **did(n't)** + **Subjekt** + **Infinitiv** und verneinte Aussagen mit **Subjekt** + **did** + **not** bzw. **n't** + **Infinitiv** (außer bei **be** als Vollverb). Achtung: **be** hat zwei **past simple**-Formen: **was** und **were**.

» Kapitel 3: Regelmäßige, unregelmäßige und reflexive Verben S. 15

I/You/He/She/It/We/You/They worked.

Did I (you, ...) work? | Didn't I (you, ...) work?
Yes, I did./No, I didn't. | I didn't work.

I/He/She/It was late. | You/We/You/They weren't late.
Was he/Were you late? | Yes, he was./No, we weren't.

Das **past progressive** setzt sich aus **was/were** + **present participle** (=**-ing**-Form) zusammen

» Kapitel 4: Infinitiv, Partizipien und Gerund S. 20

I/He/She/It was working. | You/We/You/They were working.
Was I/he/she/it working? | Weren't you/we/you/they working?
Yes, I was. | No, you weren't.

Mit dem Hilfsverb **used to** + **Infinitiv** kann man frühere, regelmäßige Handlungen oder Situationen beschreiben.

He used to play the guitar. He didn't use/used not to play the flute.

PAST PERFECT SIMPLE UND PROGRESSIVE » Übung 8–12

Das **past perfect simple** lautet für alle Personen **had + past participle** (=Infinitiv + **-ed** oder unregelmäßige Verbform).

I/You/He/She/It/We/You/They had worked.

Had I (you, ...) worked? | Hadn't I (you, ...) worked?
Yes, I had./No, I hadn't. | I hadn't worked.

Das **past perfect progressive** setzt sich zusammen aus **had + been + present participle** (= **-ing**-Form >> s.o.).

I/You/He/She/It/We/You/They had been working.

Had I (...) been working? | Hadn't I (you, ...) been working?
Yes, I had. | No, I hadn't.

» Kapitel 14: Past tense und past perfect S. 63

★ **1.** Je einer der Sätze enthält ein Verb in der falschen Form. Kreuzen Sie ihn an.

a)

☐ A I helped her with her homework.
☐ B We forgotten our tickets.
☐ C They showed us their pictures.
☐ D She swam 100 metres.

b)

☐ A I sent you a postcard.
☐ B She rang me on my mobile.
☐ C She found my book in her room.
☐ D The town lookt totally empty.

c)

☐ A I listened to his new song.
☐ B I heart all about that.
☐ C The village lost its school.
☐ D Did you hear me just now?

★ **2.** Wie lauten die **simple past**-Formen dieser verneinten Verben?

a) isn't ____________
b) can't ____________
c) doesn't go ____________
d) aren't ____________
e) don't work ____________
f) hasn't ____________

★ **3.** Das **past tense** steht auch in Einleitungssätzen der indirekten Rede. Können Sie die Formen richtig einsetzen?

a) "Do you live in Berlin?" - She ____________ (ask) me whether I live in Berlin.

b) "Don't sign the contract." - Leo ____________ (advise) me no to sign the contract.

c) "Climb the mountain." - Max ____________ (encourage) me to climb the mountain.

★ **4.** Nur eine der vier Antworten zu diesen Fragen ist korrekt formuliert. Kreuzen Sie sie an.

a) What were you doing when I knocked?

- ☐ A I was reading a magazine.
- ☐ B I am reading a magazine.
- ☐ C I have been reading a magazine.
- ☐ D I read a magazine.

b) What were you being asked to do?

- ☐ A We were being asked to help.
- ☐ B We were asking to help.
- ☐ C We have been asked to help.
- ☐ D We asked to help.

c) What else was happening in 2014?

- ☐ A A football world cup is being held.
- ☐ B A football world cup was being held.
- ☐ C A football world cup has been held.
- ☐ D A football world cup will be held.

d) Which one were you looking for?

- ☐ A I look for the red one.
- ☐ B I have looked for the red one.
- ☐ C I looked for the red one.
- ☐ D I was looking for the red one.

★ **5.** Ergänzen Sie die Lücken mit der passenden Form des **past progressive**.

	you	**he/she/it**
a) be		
b) eat		
c) forget		
d) discuss		

★★ **6.** Wie lauten diese verneinten Verben im **past progressive**?

a) It isn't ____________

b) He didn't ____________

c) We haven't eaten ____________

d) I haven't been asked ____________

★ **7.** Beantworten Sie die Fragen in ganzen Sätzen und behalten Sie die Zeit bei (**past progressive**). Beginnen Sie mit *Yes*, ...

a) Was he doing his homework?

b) Was the dog barking?

c) Were they eating sweets in the kitchen?

d) Was she crying?

e) Were they playing games?

★★ **8.** Diese Sätze mit Verben im **past perfect** sind durcheinander geraten. Bringen Sie die einzelnen Wörter in die richtige Reihenfolge.

a) I / had / one / had / a / before / all / They / got / slice of cake /.

b) heard / I / you / you / Had / news / before / already / told / the /?

c) a call / when / just / gave / come / had / you / in / me / I /.

d) had / weren't / eaten / because / we / lunch / just / hungry / We /.

★★ **9.** Bilden Sie aus den Vorgaben die verneinte Form des **past perfect simple**. Benutzen Sie Kurzformen.

a) It develops ____________________ **c)** We choose ____________________

b) They pay ____________________ **d)** He informs ____________________

★★ **10.** Können Sie die Wörter wieder in die richtige Reihenfolge bringen?

a) Our children / enjoy / horror films / to / used /.

____

b) to / use / she / Did / work / in insurance /?

____

c) never / He / be / used / very / to / ambitious /.

____

★★ **11.** Bilden Sie jeweils die korrekte Form des **past perfect progressive**.

a) receive ____________________ **c)** rise ____________________

b) try ____________________ **d)** forecast ____________________

★★★ **12.** Vervollständigen Sie die Sätze im **past simple** oder **past perfect simple**.

a) "Why did you leave so early?" – She wondered why I ____________________ so early.

b) "How do you manage to get there in time?" – She asked her how she ____________________ to get there in time.

c) "Which wine shall we take?" – He asked me which wine we ____________________.

d) "Have you been to London?" – He asked me if I ____________________ to London.

BILDUNG: FUTURE TENSES

11

WILL-FUTURE (FUTURE SIMPLE) UND FUTURE PROGRESSIVE

Bildung (alle Personen) der **simple form**: **will + Infinitiv**
Bildung (alle Personen) der **progressive form**: **will + be + present participle**

I (you, he, she, it, we, they) will / 'll go. I (...) will not / won't go.
Will I (not) / Won't I go? Yes, I will. / No, I won't.

I (...) will be / 'll be going. I (...) will not be / won't be going.
Will I (not) / Won't I be going? Yes, I will. / No, I won't.

GOING TO-FUTURE

Es wird folgendermaßen gebildet: **am / is / are + going to + Infinitiv**

I am / 'm (not) / Am I
He (she, it) is / 's (not) / Is he (not) / Isn't he } going to try.
You (we, they) are / 're (not) / Are you (not) / Aren't you

Yes, I am / he is / you are. No, I'm not / he isn't / you aren't.

FUTURE PERFECT SIMPLE UND PROGRESSIVE

Bildung (alle Ps.) der **simple form**: **will + have + past participle**
Bildung (alle Ps.) der **progressive form**: **will + have + been + present participle**

I (...) will have / 'll have gone. I (...) will not / won't have gone.
Will I (not) / Won't I have gone? Yes, I will. / No, I won't.

I (...) will / 'll have been going. I (...) will not / won't have been going.
Will I (not) / Won't I have been going? Yes, I will. / No, I won't.

FUTURE IN THE PAST

Die Hilfsverben der **future tenses** werden um eine Stufe in die Vergangenheit verschoben: will go > would go / be going, am / is / are going to try > was / were going to try, will have gone / been going > would have gone / been going

He says he will go home early. > He said he would go home early.
I am going to help her. > I was going to help her, but then I felt ill.
She'll have gone by now. > We thought that she would have gone by then.

» Kapitel 15: Future tenses, S. 70;
» Zur Bildung des present simple und progressive, die auch Zukünftiges ausdrücken können Kapitel 9, S. 37.

★ **1.** Lesen Sie den Text durch, unterstreichen Sie die fehlerhaften Futur-Formen und schreiben Sie die richtige Form darunter.

The plan for next week's class trip to London is as follows. We will all meeting

at the airport at 7.00 am for check-in at 8.00 am. If anyone goes to be late

(e.g. due to traffic) they need to call Mr. Thompson. We are due in London at

9.00 am and will spend the first day sightseeing. There wont be any time

to check into the hotel until the evening, so everyone will needs to pack as little

as possible. Mr. Thompson is going try and find a place to leave luggage,

however, before next week.

★ **2.** Schreiben Sie diese verneinten Verben ins **going to-future** um. Benutzen Sie die gängigen Kurzformen.

a) He doesn't ______

b) She doesn't mind ______

c) I don't like ______

d) We aren't ______

★ **3. Will** oder **going to**? Setzen Sie diese Sätze wieder richtig zusammen. Achten Sie auch darauf, ob es sich um eine Frage handelt.

a) will / She / in / a / be / few / eighteen / years /.

____

b) afternoon / going / this / He / play / football / is / to /.

____

c) 10 minutes / the / be / at / will / station / in / I /.

____

d) going / out / not / to / Are / come / you /?

____

e) more / it / Will / be / not / difficult /?

____

f) it / Isn't / going / finish / he / to /?

____

★ **4.** Bilden Sie vollständige Sätze im **will-future**. Achten Sie darauf, ob es sich um eine Frage handelt.

a) Dad go supermarket tomorrow.

____

b) I not forget pass on message.

____

c) You be party Friday?

____

d) She give key when you arrive.

____

e) He play match next week?

____

f) They not come on Sunday?

____

★ **5.** Von den folgenden Beispielen ist jeweils nur eines im **future progressive**. Kreuzen Sie es an.

a)

☐ A John will meet us soon.

☐ B John is meeting us soon.

☐ C John would be meeting us soon.

☐ D John will be meeting us soon.

b)

☐ A Is she going to tell the truth?

☐ B Will she be telling the truth?

☐ C Is she telling the truth?

☐ D Will she tell the truth?

c)

☐ A They will be out together.

☐ B They are going out together.

☐ C They will be going out together.

☐ D They will go out together.

d)

☐ A I won't be waiting for you.

☐ B I won't be there for you.

☐ C I'm not going to wait for you.

☐ C I won't wait for you.

e)

☐ A She is willing to enjoy her life without him.

☐ B She will enjoy her life without him.

☐ C She is going to enjoy her life without him.

☐ D She will be enjoying her life without him

★★ **6.** Füllen Sie die Lücken mit der passenden Verbform in der 3. Person Singular.

will-future	**going to-future**	**present progressive**	**future progressive**
will go			
will be			
will have			
will try			

» Kapitel 9: Bildung Present tense und present perfect S. 37

★★ **7.** Stehen diese Sätze im **future progressive** oder im **future perfect**?

(a) They won't be riding horses. * (b) Cheryl will be waiting for me. * (c) They will have eaten. * (d) They won't have played the game. * (e) Sue will have finished her work. * (f) John will be joining us. * (g) I won't be having lunch. * (h) I will have worked enough.

future progressive: ____________________

future perfect: ____________________

★★ **8.** Ordnen Sie die **question tags** auf der rechten Seite den passenden Fragen zu.

a) She wasn't going to do a thing like that,	___	**A** won't you?
b) You won't be there all day,	___	**B** was she?
c) They said they would tell me,	___	**C** would they?
d) You will have finished it by then,	___	**D** wasn't he?
e) He was meeting her at the bus stop,	___	**E** didn't they?
f) They wouldn't let us down,	___	**F** will you?

★★ **9.** Setzen Sie die Verben a)–c) ins **future perfect simple**, die Verben d)–g) ins **future perfect progressive**. Benutzen Sie die Kurzformen.

a) I will go ____________________

b) You will not see ____________________

c) It will grow ____________________

d) She will forgive ____________________

e) They will not try ____________________

f) We will understand ____________________

g) He will not sleep ____________________

★★★ **10.** Ergänzen Sie jeweils die richtige Form des **going to-future**.

a) Enough distractions! I ______________________ to start work now.

b) You told me you ______________________ to look at it before Monday.

c) He ______________________ to fly yesterday, but then he had time – so he did.

d) Did I already tell you that I ______________________ to make a film with my brother in the holidays?

e) After this accident, it looks like you ______________________ to have to be more careful in future.

f) He said they ______________________ to play for half an hour.

g) No, I certainly ______________________ to let you do that!

h) She wasn't sure if you ______________________ to join us this evening.

★★★ **11. Füllen Sie die Lücken, indem Sie die Verben übersetzen und in die jeweils angegebene Zeitform bringen.**

a) She ______________________ (treffen, past progressive) me in the evening, but then her boss needed her to stay.

b) We ______________________ (einziehen, going to-future in the past) together, but then Luke was transferred to Scotland.

c) ______________________ Linda ______________________ (für sich behalten, future progressive) her boyfriend's secret?

d) The girls ______________________ (Schwimmen gehen, future perfect simple) when you come back. You ______________________ (arbeiten, future perfect progressive) for ten hours by then.

e) Tom said he ______________________, but he didn't turn up. (helfen, will-future in the past)

PRESENT SIMPLE UND PROGRESSIVE

12

PRESENT SIMPLE

Das **present simple** verwendet man für

• regelmäßige oder gewohnheitsmäßige Handlungen und Ereignisse	He **usually** plays tennis on Friday. We **never** play badminton.
• allgemeingültige Aussagen	The day has 24 hours.
• Fahr-/Stundenpläne, Veranstaltungen, feststehende Ereignisse und Feiertage	The train arrives **at 16.35**. It's Thanksgiving **next Thursday**.
• Einleitungssätze für zeitnahes Weitergeben von Gesprochenem (indirekte Rede ohne Zeitverschiebung)	Tim **says** (that) he's ill. She **says** (that) she's lost her key.

PRESENT PROGRESSIVE

Es wird verwendet für

• Handlungen, die gerade stattfinden:	I'm diving **at the moment**.
• „zur Zeit" stattfindende, längere Handlungen:	She's diving **this week**.
• geplante/feste Vorhaben in der Zukunft:	They're diving **next Monday**.
Letztere können aber auch mit dem **present simple** ausgedrückt werden:	We <u>leave</u> tomorrow at four.

Das **present progressive** tritt meist nur bei Tätigkeits- oder Vorgangsverben auf. Verben, die einen Zustand ausdrücken, bilden normalerweise keine **progressive**-Form, es sei denn, sie drücken eine Tätigkeit aus. Sie ändern dann jedoch ihre Bedeutung:

These oranges <u>taste</u> sweet.	Diese Orangen schmecken süß.
Mary <u>is tasting</u> the soup.	Mary schmeckt die Suppe ab.

Verben ohne **-ing**-Form sind z. B. **see, hear, feel, notice, be, have, contain, possess, belong, think, believe, understand, know, want, prefer, hope, like, love, hate.**

» Kapitel 9: Bildung Present tense und present perfect S. 37;
» Kapitel 15: Future tenses S. 70

★ **1.** Ergänzen Sie die Lücken in der E-Mail mit den richtigen Verbformen.

live * hope * can * are * do * like * is * don't * am

Hello Jane!

My name ________ **(a)** Patrick and I ________ **(b)** your new penpal. I ________ **(c)** you ________ **(d)** understand my English and that you ________ **(e)** need a dictionary. I ________ **(f)** listening to music and playing tennis. What ________ **(g)** your interests? And where ________ **(h)** you live? I live in a small town near Frankfurt.

Best wishes, Patrick

» PONS Verbtabellen Plus Englisch S. 128, 52, 36, 76, 124.

★ **2.** In dieser Wortschlange verstecken sich Signalwörter und -ausdrücke für **present simple** und **progressive**. Können Sie sie finden und richtig zuordnen?

oftenthesedaysregularlynowusuallyatthemoment
sometimesalwaysthisseason never

simple: ________________________________

progressive: ________________________________

★★ **3.** Wählen Sie die passende Verbform aus.

a) We **are usually taking out/usually take out** about four or five books.

b) At the moment, I **am/am being** not sure about that.

c) She **talks/is talking** to her mother on the phone right now.

d) They **are worrying/worry** about the match this evening.

★★ **4.** Wählen Sie jeweils das passende Verb aus dem Kasten und setzen Sie es in der korrekten Zeitform **(present simple** oder **progressive)** ein.

be * need * show * take * live

a) Almost 20 million people __________ in and around New York.

b) Nobody __________ their cars today because it's snowing.

c) Tokyo __________ the biggest city in the world.

d) When a city gets large, it __________ public transport.

e) Look, a guide __________ tourists around the sights of the old town.

★★★ **5.** Setzen Sie je nach Zusammenhang das Verb im **present simple** oder **progressive** ein. Benutzen Sie die Kurzformen, die sich dabei ergeben.

a) The Carstairs __________ (usually/wash) their car once a week.

b) Hold on a second. I __________ (wash) my hands at the moment.

c) Sylvie's a vegetarian. Vegetarians __________ (not/eat) meat.

d) I __________ (dislike) going to the dentist's.

e) Joe __________ (celebrate) his fortieth birthday next Sunday.

f) The Millers' plane __________ (arrive) at 15.34.

g) Tom __________ (do) a lot of yoga these days. I __________ (think) he __________ (enjoy) it.

h) My neighbour __________ (sometimes/take care) of my garden for me.

i) That new bike __________ (belong) to Dad. He __________ (often/cycle) to work.

j) This essay __________ (take) into account all major arguments but it __________ (not/conclude) logically.

★★★ **6.** Übertragen Sie die folgenden Sätze ins Englische.

a) Ich spreche im Moment am Telefon.

b) Robbie und Ken essen gerade Äpfel.

c) Bob und Carl kochen ziemlich oft zusammen.

d) Tara mag frischen Salat – besonders im Sommer.

e) Cindy kann den Anruf nicht entgegennehmen, weil sie am Steuer sitzt.

f) Die Jungs wollen nicht hereinkommen, obwohl es regnet.

PRESENT PERFECT SIMPLE UND PROGRESSIVE

13

PRESENT PERFECT SIMPLE

Das **present perfect simple** verwendet man, um die Wirkung bzw. das Ergebnis einer vergangenen Handlung auf die Gegenwart zu beschreiben, z. B. bei

- Handlungen, die gerade erst abgeschlossen wurden **(just)**
  This cake's hot – I've **just** taken it out of the oven.
- Dingen, die noch nicht geschehen sind **(never, not ... yet)**
  We haven't received your letter **yet**.
  He's **never** seen a doctor in his life.
- Fragen, ob etwas bis jetzt schon/schon einmal passiert ist **(yet, ever)**
  Have you **ever** had an allergic reaction?
  Have they reserved a room **yet**?
- Zuständen, die bis in die Gegenwart dauern **(since, for, all day long ...)**
  I've known Marc **for** years.

Im Deutschen wird das Perfekt auch für abgeschlossene Handlungen benutzt. Im Englischen darf dafür nur das **past tense** benutzt werden!

» Kapitel 14: Past tense und past perfect S. 63

PRESENT PERFECT PROGRESSIVE

Es wird verwendet für Handlungen, die bis jetzt angedauert haben und noch weiter andauern können (häufig mit **since, for, all day** ...); es betont den Ablauf der Handlung. Bei der Übersetzung ins Deutsche verwendet man meist Präsens mit *schon*.

Dad <u>has been working</u> in the garden **all afternoon**, and he's still busy.
It<u>'s been raining</u> **since** midday.
She<u>'s been reading</u> **for** ages.

Verben, die einen Zustand ausdrücken, bilden normalerweise keine **progressive**-Form, es sei denn, sie drücken eine Tätigkeit aus.

» Kapitel 9: Bildung Present tense und present perfect S. 37

★ **1.** Sie beantworten eine E-Mail Ihrer amerikanischen Brieffreundin. Ergänzen Sie die Lücken.

painting * I've * have * moving * been * doing

Hey Jane!

Sorry it has taken me so long to reply: I've ________________ **(a)** working really hard for the next set of exams. What have you been ________________ **(b)** over the last few weeks? ________________ **(c)** also been helping my parents to repaint downstairs – we have been ________________ **(d)** furniture from room to room and ________________ **(e)** every evening for over a week now – and we still haven't finished!

What ________________ **(f)** you been doing recently?

Best, Patrick

★ **2.** Welche Zeitangaben im **present perfect** werden mit **for**, welche mit **since** gemacht? Ordnen Sie richtig zu.

2010 * years * I was a child * 24th May * ages * two hours * 3 o'clock * last year
a couple of months

since	for
________________	________________
________________	________________
________________	________________
________________	________________
________________	________________

★★ **3.** Vervollständigen Sie diese Sätze, indem Sie die richtige Form des Verbs und die passende Zeit (entweder **past simple** oder **present perfect**) auswählen.

a) Last night, I **finded/have found/found** a really funny video on the internet.

b) Look how her dog **grew/has grewn/has grown** since last time!

c) She **left/has left/leaved** for America last week.

d) He **read/has read/has readen** the morning papers for years.

» Kapitel 3: Regelmäßige, unregelmäßige und reflexive Verben S. 15

★★ **4.** Wann wird das **present perfect** gebraucht, wann das **past simple**? Ordnen Sie die Sätze einander zu. Vorsicht: Manche deutschen Sätze im Präsens benötigen im Englischen das **present perfect**.

a) Ich wohne seit fünf Jahren in London.	___	A	I haven't quarrelled with my sister for three days.
b) Ich habe letzte Woche nicht mit meiner Schwester gestritten.	___	B	Have you ever visited Iceland?
c) Hast du jemals Island bereist?	___	C	I didn't quarrel with my sister last week.
d) Ich habe fünf Jahre lang in London gelebt *(früher)*.	___	D	We did that yesterday.
e) Hast du letztes Jahr Island bereist?	___	E	Did you visit Iceland last year?
f) Ich streite seit drei Tagen nicht mehr mit meiner Schwester.	___	F	I lived in London for five years.
g) Wir haben das schon erledigt.	___	G	We've done that already.
h) Wir haben das gestern erledigt.	___	H	I've lived in London for five years.

★★★ **5.** Setzen Sie die Vorgaben in der richtigen Zeitform (**past simple**, **present perfect simple** oder **progressive**) ein. Beachten Sie Kontext und Signalwörter.

Hey Jane!

How ______________ your exams ______________ (go) **(a)** last week?

______________ you ______________ (get) **(b)** any results yet?

It ______________ (be) **(c)** a while since you last ______________ (write) **(d)**, so I'm guessing that you ______________ (work) **(e)** hard for the last few weeks. I have some exams soon, too, so I ______________ (revise) **(f)** every day. By the way, I ______________ (decide) **(g)** to take up a new hobby when my exams are finished – I'm going to learn how to play the guitar! I ______________ already ______________ (buy) **(h)** a book of songs to practice, and I ______________ just ______________ (ask) **(i)** my mum for a guitar for my birthday! ______________ you ever ______________ (consider) **(j)** learning an instrument? – Write back soon.

Best, Patrick

★★★ **6.** Übertragen Sie die folgenden Sätze ins Englische. Sie benötigen **present perfect simple** und **progressive** sowie **present simple**.

a) *Lernen Sie schon lange Deutsch?*

____

b) *Wie oft waren Sie schon in London?*

____

c) *Ich war gerade erst im Urlaub dort. Nun bin ich wieder zurück.*

____

PAST TENSE UND PAST PERFECT

14

PAST SIMPLE UND PROGRESSIVE

Das **past simple** verwendet man für

• abgeschlossene Handlungen, z. B. mit **yesterday, last ..., ...ago, in 1980**	He saw his sister **one month ago**. They went to Canada **last year**.
• regel- oder gewohnheitsmäßige Handlungen in der Vergangenheit **(always)**	We **always** went to school by bus.
• Einleitungssätze für späteres Weitergeben von Gesprochenem (indirekte Rede mit Zeitverschiebung)	Mike said that he had met Rita. He said they had talked about Jim.

Das **past progressive** verwendet man für

• Hintergrundhandlungen für kürzere, neu einsetzende Handlungen	I was reading **when** the phone rang./ **While** I was reading, the phone rang.
• gleichzeitige, vergangene Handlungen	**While** I was waiting for the bus, it was raining./ It was raining **when** I ...
• temporäre, vergangene Situationen	Mia was **temporarily** living in Paris.
• die Betonung d. Dauer einer Handlung	They were discussing **for hours**.

Frühere Gewohnheiten oder Zustände kann man auch mit Hilfe von **used to** + **Infinitiv** ausdrücken: There used to be a butcher's on that corner.

PAST PERFECT SIMPLE UND PROGRESSIVE

Das **past perfect simple** wird verwendet für

• Handlungen, die vor einem anderen, vergangenen Ereignis liegen (meist im **past simple**)	He showed me the photos he had taken in Maui **the year before**.
• mit Verben, die einen Denkvorgang ausdrücken (think, realise, ...)	When he arrived at the railway station he **realised** he had forgotten his ticket.
• Einleitungssätze für späteres Weitergeben von Gesprochenem (indirekte Rede mit Zeitverschiebung)	We missed Jim at the party. He had told Rita that he was ill and couldn't come.

Das **past perfect progressive** wird verwendet für

• längere Handlungen vor einer anderen, vergangenen Handlung, oft mit Angabe der Dauer	Tommy had been playing quietly **for an hour** when he suddenly started to cry.

» Kapitel 10: Bildung Past tense und past perfect S. 44

★ **1.** Die Dialoge stehen im **past simple**. Ordnen Sie die Antworten den passenden Fragen zu.

a) "When did you water the plants?"

b) "Did you warm up properly?"

c) "Did you play well?"

d) "Did you prepare everything for dinner?"

___ A "I played better than ever."

___ B "I watered them yesterday."

___ C "Yes, I prepared everything."

___ D "No, I think I didn't warm up long enough."

» PONS Verbtabellen Plus Englisch S. 146 (play).

★ **2.** Füllen Sie die Lücken mit den passenden Verbformen. Wann benötigen Sie das **past simple**, wann das **past progressive**?

was having * thought * brought * knocked * was explaining * patted * were having proposed * ran * was shouting

While my wife and I ________________ **(a)** lunch in the kitchen, my cat ________________ **(b)** away. I ________________ **(c)** about how nice and quiet it was in the house, when suddenly my neighbour ________________ **(d)** at the door. He ________________ **(e)** our cat back. As always, my wife ________________ **(f)** our cat while my neighbour ________________ **(g)** to me how much damage it had caused. After he had left, I ________________ **(h)** nostalgic memories of the time when we didn't have a cat. At that moment my wife ________________ **(i)** getting another cat to keep ours company.

» PONS Verbtabellen Plus Englisch S. 102, 180, 46, 152.

★ **3.** Passen diese Verbformen besser zu einem Satzbaustein in der direkten oder in der indirekten Rede? Schreiben Sie die Formen in die entsprechende Spalte.

he had tried hard * they are not here * things had changed * she will be going as well they weren't here * he has tried hard * it has improved a lot * things have changed she would be going as well * you can't make it * it had improved a lot * you couldn't make it

I know that	You said that
________________	________________
________________	________________
________________	________________
________________	________________
________________	________________
________________	________________

★ **4.** Bei diesen Sätzen fehlt entweder **when** oder **while**. Bei welchen Sätzen fehlt **when**? Kreuzen Sie sie an.

- ☐ **a)** Sara was angry ... she caught her boyfriend cheating on her.
- ☐ **b)** What were you doing ... you heard the news?
- ☐ **c)** I smoked ... we were having a break.
- ☐ **d)** ... I heard a loud thump, I stopped the car.
- ☐ **e)** ... my husband was cooking dinner, I was relaxing on the sofa.
- ☐ **f)** ... we were waiting for the train, it started to snow.
- ☐ **g)** The kids were watching TV ... their friends arrived.
- ☐ **h)** ... I came home, Sally was working.

★ **5.** Vervollständigen Sie den Text mit den passenden Verbformen. Tipp: Es handelt sich um einen Bericht über ein Ereignis in der Vergangenheit mit direkter Rede.

"What are you ____________ (look) **(a)** at?" my teacher ____________ (ask) **(b)** me. I ____________ (not/do) **(c)** know what to reply. "Nothing... I ____________ (be) **(d)** looking at my book." I didn't ____________ (want) **(e)** to say that I was too interested in the view through the window.

"Well, pay attention. You ____________ (not/do) **(f)** concentrate hard enough in my lessons," he ____________ (say) **(g)**. "I ____________ (promise) **(h)** to work harder," I ____________ (reply) **(i)**.

» PONS Verbtabellen Plus Englisch S. 130, 34, 76, 36, 188, 154.

★★ **6.** Verknüpfen Sie die Satzanfänge links sinnvoll mit den passenden Sätzen rechts im **past perfect simple** oder **progressive**.

a) He washed his hands	___	A	because he hadn't been feeling well lately.
b) Before they went shopping,	___	B	he had been training for months.
c) Sarah was afraid of her teacher	___	C	because he hadn't had time for coffee.
d) Before he won the marathon,	___	D	they had written a shopping list.
e) He was very tired at work	___	E	after he had been gardening for hours.
f) Aaron went to the doctor	___	F	though she had always done well before.

★★ **7.** Diese Sätze sind durcheinander geraten. Bringen Sie die Wörter in die richtige Reihenfolge. Achtung, es sind Sätze in indirekter Rede und Fragen dabei.

a) before / you / realise / that / Didn't / had / she / flown / never /?

____

b) on holiday / me / you / all week / been / that / told / away / had / Daniel /.

____

c) My cat / scratching / for hours / been / got back / had / the sofa / when / we /.

____

d) for / with / chatting / had / been / by / her / half an hour / I / then /.

____

e) having / Have / that / is / told / been / he / trouble / with / you / the work /?

____

f) the party / coming / Craig / heard / you / weren't / that / to /.

____

★★ **8.** Je eine der vier Antworten zu diesen Fragen enthält entweder eine falsche Formulierung oder Vergangenheitsform. Kreuzen Sie die falsche Antwort an.

a) Did you read a lot as a child?

- ☐ **A** Yes, I used to read a lot.
- ☐ **B** Yes, I read a lot of comics.
- ☐ **C** No, I never read much.
- ☐ **D** Yes, I got used to read.

b) Who used to pick you up from school?

- ☐ **A** My mother used to picked me up.
- ☐ **B** My father used to pick me up.
- ☐ **C** Granny would often pick me up.
- ☐ **D** My mother always picked me up.

c) Where did she and her family live before they moved here?

- ☐ **A** Her family used to live in Kent.
- ☐ **B** They have lived in Rio before they moved.
- ☐ **C** They were living in Maui before they moved.
- ☐ **D** They lived in Rio until last year.

d) What was your favourite child's toy?

- ☐ **A** I used to love my old teddy bear.
- ☐ **B** My favourite toy was always my doll's house.
- ☐ **C** I never had a favourite toy.
- ☐ **D** My rocking horse got used to be my favourite.

★★ **9.** Setzen Sie die Verbformen entsprechend der Zeitangaben im Satz ein.

had been having * was going * had gone * had done * did * went * were doing

Last Wednesday, I ______________ **(a)** to the shops because I needed some things. My sister ______________ **(b)** her maths homework when I came home. Yesterday, I ______________ **(c)** through my whole wardrobe by the time I realised my shorts were in the wash. Then, I ______________ **(d)** to football practice when my trainer called me and told me it was off. So I helped my sister. She ______________ **(e)** a great job on that essay last week. But she didn't tell me that she ______________ **(f)** trouble with biology.

★★★ **10.** Vervollständigen Sie die Sätze in der indirekten Rede.

a) "Why did you leave so early?" – She wondered why I ______________ so early.

b) "Do you live in Berlin?" – She asked me whether I ______________ in Berlin.

c) "How do you manage to get there in time?" – She asked her how she ______________ to get there in time.

d) "Don't sign the contract." – Leo advised me ______________ the contract.

e) "What would you like to do?" – He asked me what I ______________ to do.

f) "Have you been to London?" – He asked me if I ______________ to London.

g) "Climb the mountain." – Max encouraged me ______________ the mountain.

★★★ **11.** Setzen Sie die Verben in der richtigen Zeitform (**past simple** oder **past perfect simple**) ein. Benutzen Sie dabei Kurzformen, wenn sie sich ergeben.

a) Before their trip to France, they ______________ (not/be) on holiday together.

b) The cat ______________ (steal) my fish before I could even start to cook.

c) First, he had dinner, and then he ______________ (go) to the cinema.

d) When I ______________ (arrive) at home I realised that I ______________ (lose) my keys.

e) I ______________ (want) to travel to Norway, but I didn't have the money.

f) After they ______________ (travel) together, she ______________ (love) him even more.

g) He ______________ (pay) the bill before she could protest.

h) When Sue noticed a blue car following her, she thought that she ______________ (see) it earlier that day.

15 FUTURE TENSES

FUTURE SIMPLE (WILL-FUTURE) UND FUTURE PROGRESSIVE

• Vermutung über bevorstehendes Ereignis / zukünftige Handlung	I **hope** Sam will have a good time working in India.
• spontane Entscheidung	Oh no, I missed my bus! – I'll drive you.
• Wettervorhersage	It'll be cloudy **tomorrow** morning.
• anhaltende zukünftige Handlungen	This time **tomorrow** I'll be driving home.
• geplante Unternehmung zu einem späteren Zeitpunkt in der Zukunft	"When we're in Rome, will we be going on a tour?"

GOING TO-FUTURE

• Vorhersage eines Ereignisses aufgrund von deutlichen Anzeichen	Look, the sky is getting darker. It's going to rain.
• Plan oder Idee für ein zukünftiges Ereignis	We're going to spend our holiday in Spain this year.

PRESENT SIMPLE UND PROGRESSIVE

• feststehendes Ereignis oder Fest	Christmas Eve is on a Thursday.
• Fahrpläne, Stundenpläne	The next flight to Paris is at 7.35.
• Veranstaltungen	The concert starts at 8 p.m.
• in Nebensätzen	What will happen if it rains?
• beschlossenes Vorhaben	I'm going on a date **tonight**.
• feste Vereinbarung	We're having a barbecue **next weekend**.

FUTURE PERFECT SIMPLE UND PROGRESSIVE

• abgeschlossene Handlungen in der Zukunft	**By the time** they arrive **tomorrow** I will have completed the birthday cake.
• anhaltende Handlungen in der Zukunft, deren Dauer betont wird	My Dad will have been working on his farm **for 50 years next month**.

FUTURE IN THE PAST

• indirekte Rede mit Zeitverschiebung **(future, future perfect)**	**He said** he would call her./ **She said** she would have moved **by the end of June**.
• unerledigte Absicht	She was going to give me her address.
• feste Vereinbarung in der Vergangenheit	I was meeting her at the coffee shop **the next day.**

» Kapitel 11: Bildung Future tenses S. 49

★ **1.** Bilden Sie aus den Vorgaben das jeweils passende Verb oder Hilfsverb.

go • won't • be • will • leave • will

a) ______________ you going to the party this evening?

b) My sister ______________ be in India for one year.

c) The train ______________ at 4 pm so we meet at 3.30.

d) What is she ______________ to do while he's away?

e) Just listen! Why ______________ you let me explain?

f) In twenty years, most cars ______________ be electric.

★ **2.** Wandeln Sie diese Sätze ins Futur um. Benutzen Sie das **will-future** und alle Kurzformen, die sich ergeben.

a) I went to Mallorca for a week with my family.

____

____

b) They play football on Fridays in term time.

____

____

c) We haven't flown to New York this year.

____

____

d) He's done all of his homework today!

____

____

★★ **3.** Wie lauten die fehlenden Verbteile in diesen Sätzen über die Zukunft? Schreiben Sie sie in die Lücken.

a) I will ______________ working all summer to earn some pocket money.

b) Why is he ______________ to stop playing for the team?

c) Their plans have changed – they ______________ be coming until Monday.

d) We're not going ______________ go anywhere until this house has been cleared up!

e) If I tell you a secret, will you ______________ able to keep it?

f) Whatever ______________ we going to do without it?

g) ______________ the weather be fine tomorrow?

h) We ______________ going to the exhibition, but I felt ill that day.

★★ **4.** Alle Aussagen beziehen sich auf die Zukunft. Es werden aber unterschiedliche Zeiten verwendet (**will-future, going to-future, present simple** und **present progressive**). Mit welcher Absicht werden die Sätze gesprochen? Ordnen Sie zu.

a) The lesson starts at 8.30.	___	A Plan oder Idee
b) Mike's birthday is on a Monday this year.	___	B Vermutung
c) Ben will probably meet nice people on his trip.	___	C feststehendes, Ereignis, vom Sprecher nicht beeinflussbar
d) It'll be sunny tomorrow morning.	___	D Stundenplan
e) Sandra is going to have a party next Saturday.	___	E fest beschlossenes Vorhaben, alles ist bereits organisiert
f) Sandra is having a party next Saturday.	___	F Wettervorhersage

★★ **5. Schreiben Sie die richtigen Verbformen in die Lücken. Die Zeitangaben helfen Ihnen zu erkennen, um welche Zukunftsform es sich in welchem Satz handelt.**

will have read * will have travelled * won't have done * will find * was going to come
am going to finish * won't worry * will go out

a) Tomorrow, I ________________ my homework before I log on to social networking sites.

b) You know what? I think I ________________ this evening. I've got nothing better to do!

c) They ________________ it very difficult to beat last year's winners.

d) I did not know that he ________________. I thought he had already seen the film.

e) Just think of it! By this time next year, your brother ________________ around the world on his gap year.

f) At this rate, you ________________ even the half of it before she gets back!

g) She ________________ too much about her exams, will she?

h) I promise: I ________________ the whole thing before we next meet.

★★ **6. Jeweils eine der drei Antworten zu diesen Fragen ist in ihrer Schreibweise falsch. Kreuzen Sie sie an.**

a) What about that concert this evening?

☐ **A** Sounds great, but I won't be going.

☐ **B** No. Who'll be playing, then?

☐ **C** My sister's got tickets, so well be going.

b) When can you finish it by?

☐ **A** I should've finished it by midday.

☐ **B** I wont have got through it until Monday.

☐ **C** I'll have done it before the end of the week.

» Kapitel 11: Bildung Future tenses S. 49

★★ **7.** **Ergänzen Sie die Lücken mit den passenden Formen aus dem Kasten.**

will be looking * will have * would look * will have looked * will look
will have been looking * will have to look

a) As of next week, my parents ______________ for a new house for two years!

b) She says she ______________ at it for us by Monday.

c) It is so well hidden that he ______________ very carefully to find it.

d) He ______________ after her if she gets ill.

e) They say they ______________ after our house while we're away.

f) The manager says he ______________ the damage looked at by the end of the week.

g) Tom said he ______________ over the house before we put in an offer for it.

» PONS Verbtabellen Plus Englisch S. 130-131 (look).

★★ **8.** **Diese Fragen und Antworten sind durcheinander geraten. Können Sie die Reaktionen rechts den passenden Fragen und Behauptungen zuordnen?**

a) I won't be able to help.	___	**A** Yes, I was.
b) Will he be coming with you?	___	**B** Does it?
c) Isn't she going out tonight?	___	**C** No, he won't.
d) We are going to go swimming on Saturday.	___	**D** No, it won't.
e) Won't it be too much?	___	**E** Are you?
f) It's going to be a real challenge.	___	**F** Won't you?
g) The plane arrives at 3.30 pm.	___	**G** Yes, she is.
h) Weren't you meeting her that evening?	___	**H** Is it?

★★★ **9.** Ergänzen Sie die Sätze mit den passenden Verbformen im **future perfect** oder **future perfect progressive**. Benutzen Sie bei Verneinungen die Kurzformen.

a) At the end of this month, I ______________ (look) for a Saturday job for five weeks – and I ______________ (find) anything!

b) It's hard to imagine, but by this time next year, we ______________ (travel) for ten whole months!

c) I'm going to offer it to him one more time – he ______________ (probably, think) it over again by now.

d) What do you think ______________ (happen) to the world by 2020? Do you think the ice caps ______________ (melt)?

★★★ **10.** Vervollständigen Sie diese E-Mail an ihre amerikanische Brieffreundin.

will • been • had • going • travelling • would • be • need • forgotten • able • have

Hi there Jane! I thought the e-mail I wrote you last week **(a)** ______________ be the last one before I left, but there are a few things I **(b)** ______________ **(c)** ______________ to ask you. Firstly, will I **(d)** ______________ to bring any adapters? And will we **(e)** ______________ going skiing? If so, **(f)** ______________ you be **(g)** ______________ to lend me some skis? Lastly, you mentioned that we were **(h)** ______________ to have a look around Denver straight after you pick me up at the airport, but could we change plans? I will **(i)** ______________ **(j)** ______________ **(k)** ______________ for ten hours by then! – Best, Patrick

★★★ **11.** Können Sie die deutschen Verben in die korrekte englische Zeitform übertragen? Achten Sie dafür auf Angaben zu Zeit und Dauer in den Sätzen.

a) When they take their final exams, they ____________________ (werden gelernt haben) English for at least eight years.

b) What about Sunday? – I can't, I ____________________ (gehe) to the theatre that evening.

c) By the time my cousin comes back, she ____________________ (wird gereist sein) over 10,000 miles in four weeks.

d) The weather forecast says it ____________________ (wird regnen) all afternoon.

e) If you ____________________ (nur, warten) one second, I can pass you over to her.

f) If I can still make it by eight, you ____________________ (wirst nicht gewartet haben) too long, will you?

g) They ____________________ (werden spielen) on Friday between four and six, will you come and watch?

GEBRAUCH DES CONDITIONAL

16

CONDITIONAL SIMPLE UND PROGRESSIVE

Das **conditional simple** wird gebraucht für

• Vorschläge, Ansichten, noch unsichere Ereignisse oder Handlungen	Jim: "Which cake would you choose?" Carol: "I'd take that one."
• **if**-Sätze vom Typ II (**if**-Nebensatz im **past simple** enthält eine eher unwahrscheinliche Bedingung)	**If** you **did** more sport, you would lose weight.
• höfliche Fragen und Bitten	Would you like a cup of tea?

Das **conditional progressive** wird gebraucht, um

• den Verlauf einer im Moment (theoretisch) möglichen Handlung zu betonen.	If I **were*** on holiday, I would be swimming in the sea. (* **were-subjunctive** s. Tipp)

CONDITIONAL PERFECT SIMPLE UND PROGRESSIVE

Das conditional perfect simple wird gebraucht für

• **if**-Sätze Typ III (**if**-Nebensatz im **past perfect** mit unerfüllbarer Bedingung)	I'd have called him back **if** he **had left** his number.
• Handlungen u. Ereignisse, die in der Vergangenheit nicht geschehen sind	I wouldn't have thought of that. I would have been too afraid for that.

Das **conditional perfect progressive** wird gebraucht für

• gedachte, nicht mehr realisierbare Handlungen und Ereignisse in der Vergangenheit, wobei ihre Dauer betont wird (oft mit **if**-Sätzen Typ III).	Where do you think you would have been living **for the last five years** if you hadn't had your houseboat?

In Bedingungssätzen, in Nebensätzen nach **wish** und **suppose** sowie in bestimmten, formelhaften Ausdrücken wird der **subjunctive** verwendet.

If I were you, I would go. **(were-subjunctive)** – *Wäre ich du, würde ich gehen.*
I **wish** the day were over. **(were-subjunctive)** – *Ich wünschte, der Tag wäre um.*
Long live the King. (**present subjunctive** = Infinitiv) – *Lang lebe der König.*

» Kapitel 8: Conditional S. 33; » Kapitel 18: Gebrauch der Modalverben S. 88

★ **1.** Ordnen Sie die Sätze den Bildern zu. Dann schreiben Sie jeweils zu den Sätzen, welche Sprechabsicht aus dem Kasten dazu passt.

höfliche Vorschläge oder Anregungen • Bedingungssätze (if-Sätze) • höfliche Bitten
höfliche Fragen

___ **a)** Could you give me your number, please?

____

A

___ **b)** Which cake would you choose?

____

B

___ **c)** If my alarm clock didn't ring,
I would never get up in time.

____

C

___ **d)** Would you like to talk about your problem?

____

D

★ **2. Verbinden Sie die Satzanfänge und -enden wieder richtig miteinander.**

a) If I asked you,	___ **A** I'm going to buy a Ferrari!
b) If he rings,	___ **B** I'll switch on the computer.
c) When I'm rich,	___ **C** would you come with me?
d) If I were rich,	___ **D** I would spend all my money.
e) When I get home,	___ **E** will you pick up for me?

★★ **3.** Unterstreichen Sie in diesen **conditional**-Sätzen die passende Form.

a) You **wouldn't/couldn't** know where to buy one, would you?

b) **Should/Could** you help me with these bags, please?

c) Are you telling me that you **wouldn't/must** cheat in an exam if you could?

d) If he **gave/gives** me the chance, I would explain what happened to him.

e) **Will/Did** the others do the washing up if Jaspers does the cooking?

f) If Sally **would be/is** nice to her little brother, she'll get chocolate.

g) If we were able to sell our flat for a good price, we'**ll/'d** buy a small house.

★★ **4.** Sie beantworten eine E-Mail ihrer amerikanischen Brieffreundin. Ergänzen Sie die Lücken.

would * sitting * do * sent * going * find * went * wouldn't * could * be

Hi there Jane!

Great to hear from you. I'm so glad your exams ______________ **(a)** well. When ______________ **(b)** you get your results? I'm ______________ **(c)** to be ______________ **(d)** my exams next week, so keep your fingers crossed for me. On that matter, I was wondering if I ______________ **(e)** ask you a favour? If I ______________ **(f)** you one of my English essays, ______________ **(g)** you ever ______________ **(h)** able to look over it and tell me if you ______________ **(i)** any mistakes? I hope that ______________ **(j)** be too much trouble!

Best, Patrick

★★ **5.** Ergänzen Sie die Lücken mit der jeweils passenden Form. Bei einigen – aber nicht allen – Sätzen benötigen Sie das **conditional**.

a) If I ______________ (can), I would go on holiday every year.

b) I ______________ (go) on holiday this summer if I can.

c) What would you say if I ______________ (tell) you that she's coming tonight?

d) When they arrive, I ______________ (meet) them at the station and then we ______________ all ______________ (go) to a restaurant.

e) If it ______________ (not be) so cold, I would go out for a run.

f) What ______________ you ______________ (say) in the speech if you were me?

g) Whenever he is allowed, he ______________ (go) to the shops.

h) If he ______________ (be allowed to), he would go to the shops more often.

i) I would do it if I ______________ (must/have to), of course!

» PONS Verbtabellen Plus Englisch S. 52, 100, 136, 36, 154, 138.

★★ **6.** Mit welcher der beiden Zeitformen können Sie jeweils die Lücken in diesen **conditional**-Sätzen richtig ergänzen? Markieren Sie sie.

a) He would **have lain/be lying** in the sun by now if the plane hadn't been cancelled.

b) I would **have lied/have been lying** if I had said that I wasn't interested.

c) She wouldn't **have said/have been saying** anything if she didn't want to, you know.

d) They will **play/be playing** on Friday. Will you come and watch?

e) If I do turn up by eight, you won't **wait/have been waiting** too long, will you?

f) If you'll just **wait/be waiting** one second, I can pass you over to her.

★★ **7.** Eine der Antworten passt nicht zu der jeweiligen Frage. Kreuzen Sie sie an.

a) What would you do with the money?

☐ **A** I would have spent it all at once.

☐ **B** I would donate it to charity.

☐ **C** I would put it in the bank.

b) What would he say about it?

☐ **A** I don't know what he'd say.

☐ **B** I'm not sure what he'd say.

☐ **C** I think he would have been furious.

c) What would she have done if she had known?

☐ **A** She would be very upset by it.

☐ **B** She would have gone straight over there!

☐ **C** She wouldn't have gone to the party, that's for sure.

d) What would you have done without your bike?

☐ **A** I would have had to walk.

☐ **B** I would have to walk.

☐ **C** I would have taken the bus.

★★ **8.** Setzen Sie die fehlenden Zeitformen ein.

had * would go * ate * would lead * wouldn't know * were * did * would buy

a) If I had as much money as you, I ______________ a fast and expensive car.

b) I wouldn't go to work by train if I ______________ the money for a taxi.

c) If I were you, I ______________ a completely different life.

d) If you ______________ more sports, you would lose weight.

e) If we lived together, I ______________ crazy.

f) If you ______________ more fruit, you'd feel a lot better.

g) I would invite your friends around more often if they ______________ nicer.

h) You ______________ what to do if I didn't give you advice.

★★★ **9.** Bringen Sie die Wörter dieser **conditional**-Sätze in die richtige Reihenfolge. Beachten Sie, ob es sich um vergangene Ereignisse handelt oder um etwas, das noch passieren könnte.

a) had / She / the money / buy / if / would / she / a car /.

____

b) have / the game / played / lost / if / Daniel / had / I / would /.

____

c) would / it / have / if / weren't / gone / my lovely cat / for / mad / I /.

____

d) braked / in time / I / I / If / have / had / , / rabbit / the / seen / would /.

____

★★★ **10.** Vervollständigen Sie diese Sätze, indem Sie die Verben im **conditional perfect simple** oder im **conditional perfect progressive** konjugieren.

a) It ____________ (be) great to see you, but we were away.

b) We ____________ (lie) in the sun by now if we hadn't missed that flight. If only we had woken up earlier!

c) She ____________ (want to go) to go if she had known about it.

d) He ____________ (can go) on the trip to Africa if he had got all his vaccinations done.

e) They ____________ (must pull out) of the tournament if the referee had noticed how badly they were cheating.

f) That book ____________ (still, sit) on the shelves if it hadn't been for all the press coverage.

★★★ **11.** Welche Satzteile passen sinnvoll zueinander? Ordnen Sie zu und schreiben Sie dann die richtige Zeitform des in Klammern angegebenen Verbs in die Lücke. Benutzen Sie die Kurzformen, wenn sie sich ergeben.

a) This accident ______________________ (not/happen)

b) If you had done more sport,

c) If Anne ______________________ (not buy) the drinks,

d) Would you have failed the exam

e) If we had been able to afford it,

f) If I ______________________ (not/fall) pregnant,

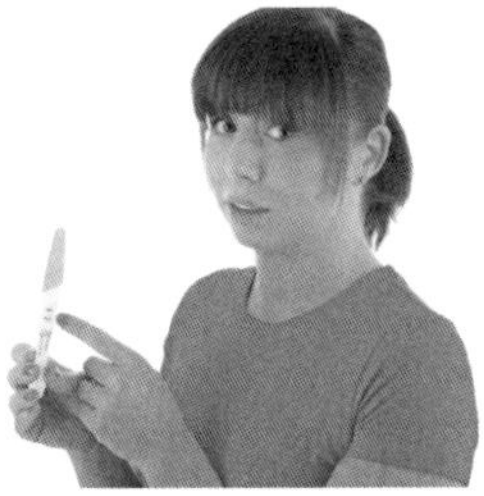

____ **A** we ______________________ (stay) longer.

____ **B** we couldn't have held the party.

____ **C** I would have left you long ago.

____ **D** if you had been more careful.

____ **E** if you ______________________ (study) harder?

____ **F** you ______________________ (lose) weight.

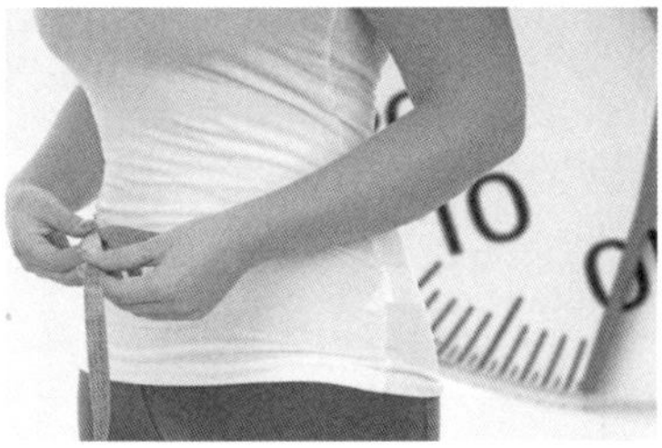

★★★ **12.** Vervollständigen Sie diese Sätze mit der richtigen Form des Modalverbs im **conditional perfect**.

a) It's just what he ________________ (want).

b) If you hadn't been there, we ________________ (not can achieve) what we did.

c) If they had come, we ________________ (must find) a larger room.

d) ________________ (they/may go out) together if you had known their plans?

e) As far as grandma was concerned, we ________________ (should eat) fish every day.

★★★ **13.** In diesen **subjunctive**-Sätzen fehlen einige Verben. Aus dem Kontext können Sie entnehmen, welches Wort hier fehlt.

a) God ____________ the Queen!

b) If I ____________ you, I would be a little more considerate.

c) I am going to have to request that he ____________ that information to himself.

d) If only my grandmother ____________ still alive today.

e) Heaven ____________ us!

f) If it ____________ only a matter of money, there would be no problem.

g) Would you fill in for me if I ____________ able to come?

h) I insist that your parents ____________ informed.

i) It is necessary that the president ____________ us permission to do so.

j) If she ____________ leaving, we would have heard about it.

STELLUNG DES VERBS IM SATZ

17

Ein Satz besteht mindestens aus Subjekt und Prädikat. Das Subjekt steht in englischen Aussagesätzen vor dem Prädikat. Ist ein Objekt vorhanden, steht es nach dem Prädikat, d. h. die wichtigste Regel zum Satzbau im Englischen lautet:

Subjekt –	**Prädikat –**	**Objekt (S – P – O)**	
I	know	(her).	*Ich weiß. / Ich kenne sie.*
He	can help	you.	*Er kann dir helfen.*
Mike	hasn't found	his key.	*Mike hat seinen Schlüssel nicht gefunden.*

Diese Regel gilt auch für Nebensätze. Achten Sie auf den Unterschied zum Satzbau im Deutschen! Weiteres zur Satzstellung bei Verben mit zwei Objekten und **phrasal verbs** finden Sie unter » Kapitel 21: Verben und Ergänzungen, S. 97

Adverbien der unbestimmten Zeit und Häufigkeit (**usually, often, always, never** etc.) stehen **zwischen** Subjekt und Prädikat, wenn das Prädikat aus einem Wort besteht, sonst **nach dem 1. Hilfsverb**:

Mike **often** cooks dinner on Sunday. — *Mike kocht oft das Abendessen am Sonntag.*
He has **always** enjoyed cooking. — *Er hat schon immer gern gekocht.*

In Fragen rückt das 1. Hilfsverb vor das Subjekt. Ist kein Hilfsverb vorhanden, steht eine Form von **do** vor dem Subjekt. Fragewörter stehen vor dem Hilfsverb am Satzanfang.

Do you often cook together? — *Kocht ihr oft zusammen?*
When did you have the idea? — *Wann hattet ihr die Idee?*

In Bestätigungsfragen (= **question tags**) und Kurzsätzen mit **so** bzw. **nor/neither** steht das Hilfsverb bzw. eine Form von **do** ebenfalls vor dem Subjekt.

Jill is working, isn't she? — *Jill arbeitet gerade, nicht wahr/stimmt's?*
Dad won't be late, will he? — *Papa wird nicht zu spät kommen, oder?*
The kids are tired. – **So** am I. — *... – Ich auch.*
I don't like that restaurant on the corner. – **Neither / Nor** do I. – *... Ich auch nicht.*

Im förmlichen Stil kann eine Umkehrung (= Inversion) der normalen Satzstellung - wie im Fragesatz - auftreten, wenn der Satz mit einem negativen Adverb beginnt. In der Umgangssprache verwendet man eher die normale Wortstellung.

Inversion: **Hardly** had she left the car when she was robbed.
Normale Wortstellung: She had **hardly** left the car ...
Inversion: **Not only** did they take her handbag, but also her watch.
Normale Wortstellung: They did**n't only** take ...

★ **1.** Bringen Sie die Wörter der Sätze unten in die richtige Reihenfolge. Beachten Sie dabei die Wortstellung im Englischen: Subjekt – Verb – (Objekt).

a) painting / Claire / is /.

____

b) a picture / Claire / is painting / for Tim /.

____

c) Benjamin / in Germany / doesn't / live /.

____

d) went / yesterday / Tom / to Dublin /.

____

e) been / has / Annette / to South Africa / never /.

____

★★ **2.** Formulieren Sie die passenden Bestätigungsfragen (**question tags**) zu den angegebenen Sätzen aus Übung 1. Achten Sie darauf, ob der Satz verneint ist.

a) Claire is painting, *isn't she?* **b)** ..., ______________?

c) ..., ______________ **d)** ..., ______________?

★★ **3.** Ergänzen Sie die Kurzsätze entweder mit **so** oder **nor** bzw. **neither** und dem passenden Verb.

a) I am feeling hungry! – *So am* ______________ I.

b) I can smell coffee. – ______________ I.

c) Carl likes porridge for breakfast, and ______________ Betty.

d) Lisa and Paul aren't coming tonight. – ______________ Jill and Mike.

★★ **4.** Hier sind die Antworten gegeben – aber wie lautet jeweils die Frage dazu? Fragen Sie nach dem unterstrichenen Satzteil, falls vorhanden.

a) Mary likes camping.

____

b) I would like to go <u>in August</u>.

____

c) They've been to <u>San Francisco</u>.

____

★★ **5.** Die folgenden Adverbien haben alle eine negative Bedeutung. Ordnen Sie die Buchstaben richtig.

a) l y r b a e ____________ **b)** r e e n v ____________

c) r s l a e y c c ____________ **d)** r h y a d l ____________

e) h e e r n o w ____________ **f)** e r l y r a ____________

g) n i e r e h t ____________ **h)** d m l s o e ____________

★★★ **6.** In förmlicher Sprache ist eine andere Wortstellung möglich, wenn ein negatives Adverb am Satzanfang steht. Setzen Sie die Sätze entsprechend zusammen.

a) she / started / Hardly / when / had / the house / left / it / to rain /.

____

b) I / such / did / Never / a crowd of people / see /.

____

c) looked / although / the car key / Nowhere / to be found / I / was / everywhere /.

____

18 GEBRAUCH DER MODALVERBEN

Mit den Modalverben können verschiedene Sprechabsichten oder auch Annahmen des Sprechenden ausgedrückt werden. Beachten Sie, dass die meisten Modalverben nur im **present tense** existieren, d. h. dass man in anderen Zeitformen Ersatzformen verwenden muss. » Kapitel 2: Modalverben S. 12
Aussagen können auch mit **modal phrases** wie z. B. **be meant to** + Infinitiv (Absicht), **be obliged to** + Infinitiv (Verpflichtung) modifiziert werden.

höfliche Fragen, Bitten bzw. Wünsche, höfliche Vorschläge: **can**, *höflicher:* **could**, **shall** (**I/we** ... ?), **would like to**	Can/Could you help me in the garden? Shall we meet tomorrow at six? Would you like me to drive you home?
Bereitschaft/Weigerung: **will, won't, would, wouldn't**	Will/Would you clear the table while I'm preparing the dessert? Claire wouldn't give the doll to her.
Verbot: **mustn't, can't, may not; be not allowed to**	You mustn't forget your keys! They won't be allowed to drink alcohol.
Erlaubnis: **may, might, can, could; be allowed to**	Students may use a dictionary in the exam. You can put your bag over there.
Vermutung: **may, might, must, will, should, ought to,** *starke Vermutung i. d. Gegenwart:* **modal** + **be** + **-ing**-Form, *Vermutung über vergangene Ereignisse bzw. nicht eingetroffene Möglichkeiten:* **modal + have + past participle**	That must/might/will/should be Lara at the door. You must be joking! I must have lost my keys. You could have met John if you hadn't been working so long.
Rat, Ermahnung, Pflicht/Zwang: **should, ought to, must,** *nur Fragen:* **need; have to, be supposed to;** *modal phrase:* **be obliged to**	You must be careful! Need I come to the police office? He was supposed to call me yesterday. They were obliged to replace the loss.
keine Notwendigkeit: **needn't; not have to**	You needn't worry, it's all taken care of. Luckily, she didn't have to change trains.
Fähigkeit: **can, could; be able to**	I can understand a bit of French.
Kritik: **could + Infinitiv, could + have + past participle**	She could be a bit friendlier. You could have told me about the exam!
Fehler, Versäumnis: **should /ought to + have + past participle**	They should /ought to have been more careful.

★ **1.** Ordnen Sie die Sätze den passenden Bildern zu. Welche Sprechabsichten oder Annahmen aus dem Kasten drücken die Sätze jeweils aus? Schreiben Sie sie dazu.

Fähigkeit/Unfähigkeit • Verbot • Angebot • Bereitschaft • Rat/Ermahnung/Pflicht

A

B

C

D

E

___ **a)** Will you help me in the garden, please?

___

___ **b)** I would like to water the flowers.

___

___ **c)** They ought to be very careful.

___

___ **d)** She can't stop buying clothes.

___

___ **e)** You mustn't eat fast food.

___

★ **2.** Die Fragen links und die **question tags** rechts sind durcheinander geraten. Ordnen Sie sie wieder einander zu.

a) I shouldn't have done that, ___ A shouldn't I?

b) I haven't had to do much about it, ___ B mustn't I?

c) I probably should have apologised, ___ C have I?

d) I must have forgotten that, ___ D should I?

★★ **3.** Formulieren Sie jeweils die fehlenden Kurzantworten und verwenden Sie dabei die Kurzformen, wenn möglich. Tipp: Es sind auch höfliche Fragen dabei.

a) Will Sarah come to my party? Yes, *she will*. /No, *she won't*.

b) Would you like something to drink? Yes, ______. /No, ______.

c) Can you fix my broken car? Yes, ______. /No, ______.

d) May I use your mobile? Yes, ______. /No, ______.

e) Is she able to care for the baby? Yes, ______. /No, ______.

f) Must I keep this secret? Yes, ______. /No, ______.

g) Do you want to wait here until it stops raining? Yes, ______. /No, ______.

h) Wouldn't you have agreed with him? Yes, ______. /No, ______.

i) Need I make an appointment? Yes, ______. /No, ______.

j) Were they allowed to stay up late? Yes, ______. /No, ______.

k) Did you have to pay extra for the bag? Yes, ______. /No, ______.

★★ **4.** Können Sie anhand der Angaben in Klammern jeweils das gesuchte englische Modalverb (oder eine Ersatzform) im **present tense** einsetzen?

a) She ______ *(ist nicht in der Lage)* do the task.

b) Her son ______ *(hat die Erlaubnis)* go out on Friday.

c) ______ *(würdest - Bereitschaft)* you do me a favour and wash the car?

d) You ______ *(solltest nicht - Ratschlag)* read the letter.

e) The children ______ *(dürfen nicht - Verbot)* open that door.

f) I ______ *(muss - innerer Zwang)* clean the kitchen.

★★★ **5. Welcher Satz passt nicht dazu? Kreuzen Sie ihn an.**

a) Mit Modalverben kann etwas Irreales in der Vergangenheit ausgedrückt werden.

☐ **A** Tim could have written another book. ☐ **B** He can't have killed his wife.

☐ **C** She should have apologized to her. ☐ **D** They wouldn't have left their child inside.

b) Mit Modalverben kann Höflichkeit ausgedrückt werden.

☐ **A** Could you open the door, please? ☐ **B** Can I go out tonight?

☐ **C** Would you like a glass of water? ☐ **D** Could you help me?

c) Mit Modalverben kann eine Vermutung ausgedrückt werden.

☐ **A** He might be able to repair the car. ☐ **B** Anna must finish her essay first.

☐ **C** Jenny must have missed the bus. ☐ **D** She may not be home.

d) Mit Modalverben können Wünsche ausgedrückt werden.

☐ **A** The kids want to go to the zoo. ☐ **B** They will sell the house.

☐ **C** We wish to speak to the manager. ☐ **D** She would like to come with us.

e) Mit Modalverben kann Kritik ausgedrückt werden.

☐ **A** Matt could have put his bike away. ☐ **B** Gran, you could have called me.

☐ **C** She could be more careful. ☐ **D** She might have missed the bus.

f) Mit Modalverben können starke Vermutungen ausgedrückt werden.

☐ **A** Kim must be lying. ☐ **B** Carol may be still working.

☐ **C** They are driving home right now. ☐ **D** Jeff could be surfing.

» PONS Verbtabellen Plus Englisch S. 52, S. 138.

19 GEBRAUCH DES IMPERATIVS

Der Imperativ wird besonders verwendet bei
- Einladungen
- Aufforderungen
- Hinweisschildern
- Verboten
- Ermahnungen

Have a cup of coffee.	*Trink/Trinken Sie eine Tasse Kaffee!*
Be careful with my car.	*Sei/Seien Sie vorsichtig mit meinem Auto!*
Don't be late.	*Komm/Kommen Sie nicht zu spät!*
Please wait here.	*Bitte warte/warten Sie hier!*
Don't block this door.	*Blockieren Sie nicht diese Tür!*
Never lie to me.	*Lüg/Lügen Sie mich niemals an!*

Anders als im Deutschen enden Aufforderungssätze im Englischen mit einem Punkt. Nur bei besonders betonten Befehlen oder Ausrufen wird ein Ausrufezeichen gesetzt.

Stop! There's a car coming.	*Halt! Da kommt ein Auto.*

Bezieht sich der Sprechende selbst in die Aufforderung mit ein, wird die Formulierung **let's** + Infinitiv bzw. **let's not** + Infinitiv verwendet.

Die Vollform **let us** + Infinitiv wird nur im förmlichen Stil verwendet.

Let's go and have a drink.	*Gehen wir ...*
Oh no, let's not go out tonight. I'd like to watch a film.	*... gehen wir lieber nicht ...*
Let us pray.	*Lasset uns beten.*

Ein zusätzliches **do** kann man verwenden, wenn man nachdrücklich um etwas bitten will:

Do please sit.	*Setz dich/setzt euch/Setzen Sie sich doch bitte!*
Do come in.	*Komm/Kommt/Kommen Sie doch bitte herein!*

» Zur Bildung siehe Kapitel 6: Imperativ S. 26

★ **1.** Welches Foto passt zu welchem Satz? Ordnen Sie zu.

A

B

C

D

___ **a)** Don't smoke in this area.

___ **b)** Mind the gap.

___ **c)** Hi. Come in and make yourself at home.

___ **d)** Talk about your problems.

★★ **2.** In welchen Situationen wird der Imperativ verwendet? Sehen Sie sich die vier Beispiele in Übung 1 nochmals an und schreiben Sie sie auf.

___

★★★ **3.** Übersetzen Sie die folgenden Sätze ins Englische.

a) *Im Notfall rufen Sie 112.*

___

b) *Unterschreiben Sie hier.*

___

c) *Nehmen Sie doch bitte Platz.*

___

d) *Lass uns nicht zu spät zurückkommen.*

___

20 LEICHT VERWECHSELBARE VERBEN UND VERBEN IN FESTEN WENDUNGEN

LEICHT VERWECHSELBARE VERBEN

Sogenannte **false friends** ähneln deutschen Wörtern im Aussehen, haben jedoch oft eine ganz andere Bedeutung. Hier einige Beispiele:

become – ~~bekommen~~ *werden:*	Katie wants to become a teacher.
spend – ~~spenden~~ *ausgeben:*	Mr Parker spends a lot of time outdoors.
wonder – ~~sich wundern~~ *sich etw. fragen*	I wonder what's happened to my glasses.

Verbpaare oder -gruppen, die ähnlich funktionieren, aber unterschiedlich gebraucht werden, sind z. B.:

borrow/lend	• *sich etwas borgen/etwas an jdn. verleihen*
fit/match/suit	• *passen bzgl. Größe/Farbe/vom Aussehen her „stehen"*
remember/remind	• *sich erinnern/jdn. an etwas erinnern*

This t-shirt fits me. It's my size. This scarf matches my hat. It's the same colour.
I can't remember the date. Can you remind me to water the plants?

VERBEN IN FESTEN WENDUNGEN

Einige englische Verben werden in Anlehnung an deutsche Ausdrucksweisen häufig falsch verwendet. z. B.:

Gut gemacht!	Well ~~made~~ done!
Ich bekomme ein Baby!	I'm ~~becoming~~ having a baby!
Er hat schlimme Erfahrungen gemacht.	He's ~~made~~ had some bad experiences.

Bei der Übersetzung bestimmter englischer Verben oder verbaler Ausdrücke (z. B. Verb + Adjektiv), die persönliche Einstellungen ausdrücken, werden im Deutschen Adverbien verwendet, z. B.

Julie is fond of singing. She likes riding, too.	*... gern ...*
Tom hates writing e-mails,	*... sehr ungern ...*
he prefers making phone calls.	*... lieber ...*
I hope you have a great time.	*Hoffentlich ...*
The weather is likely to stay fine.	*... wahrscheinlich ...*

» Kapitel 21: Verben und Ergänzungen S. 97

★ **1.** Achtung, **false friends**! Welche der beiden Übersetzungen ist jeweils korrekt?

a) spare ☐ **A** *sparen* ☐ **B** *verschonen*

b) overhear ☐ **A** *zufällig mithören* ☐ **B** *überhören*

c) become ☐ **A** *bekommen* ☐ **B** *werden*

d) wonder ☐ **A** *sich wundern* ☐ **B** *sich fragen*

e) irritate ☐ **A** *verärgern* ☐ **B** *irritieren*

f) blame ☐ **A** *blamieren* ☐ **B** *beschuldigen*

g) mob ☐ **A** *umringen* ☐ **B** *mobben*

★★ **2.** Welches Verb ist das Richtige? Wählen Sie aus.

a) Sam always tries to **overtake/take over** cars in front of him. He's crazy.

b) Traffic lights are **controlled/steered** by computers nowadays.

c) Carol **donates/spends** too much money on clothes and perfume.

d) Mr Boyden will **oversee/overlook** the group's transition to a listed company.

e) Did you **reclaim/complain** to the shop about the damaged shirt they sold you?

f) The electrician **checked/proved** all the cables last week.

★★ **3.** Tragen Sie die richtige Form von **get** oder **have** (oder beides) ein.

a) Sie bekommt ihr zweites Kind. – She is ____________ her second child.

b) Er hat viele Geschenke bekommen. – He has ____________ a lot of presents.

c) Wollen wir etwas trinken? – Shall we ____________ a drink?

d) Ich schlage vor, wir lassen uns eine Pizza liefern. – I suggest we

____________ a pizza delivered.

★★ **4.** An welche Stelle gehört welches Verb? Setzen Sie es jeweils in der richtigen Form ein.

a) Can I ______________ your car? – No, but I can ______________ you my bike. (lend, borrow)

b) Mum, the postman is ______________ a parcel for our neighbours. – They're out. Tell him we'll ______________ it to them when they're back. (take, bring)

c) Joy's ______________ a red scarf and gloves today. She's ______________ a handbag and a coat. (wear, carry)

d) I was ______________ to the news when I ______________ some cats fight outside. (hear, listen)

e) I can't ______________ his name. Can you ______________ me to note it down later so I'll know next time I see him? (remind, remember)

f) Our profits have ______________ this year, so my boss has ______________ my salary, too. (raise, rise)

g) Jenny ______________ that she had a new job. – Yes, she ______________ me all about it. (say, tell)

★★★ **5.** Übertragen Sie die folgenden Sätze ins Deutsche.

a) Frank loves hiking in the mountains.

____

b) I'm afraid I haven't got time to meet you on Friday.

____

c) We happened to meet the Scotts at the exhibition.

____

Phrasal verbs sind Verben, die fest mit mindestens einer Präposition oder einem kurzen Adverb verbunden sind. Viele Verben können mit verschiedenen Präpositionen bzw. Adverbien stehen. Sie haben dann ganz verschiedene Bedeutungen, die sich aus der Bedeutung des Verbs alleine nicht ableiten lassen. Die wichtigsten **phrasal verbs** finden Sie in den » PONS Verbtabellen Plus Englisch, S. 206–207.

He got off the bus.	*Er stieg aus dem Bus aus.*
We get on with our neighbours.	*Wir kommen mit unseren Nachbarn zurecht.*
She quickly got over their separation.	*Sie kam schnell über ihre Trennung hinweg.*

Manche **phrasal verbs** wie **look up** können getrennt werden, wenn das Objekt ein Substantiv ist. Sie müssen sogar getrennt werden, wenn das Objekt ein Pronomen ist. Einige **phrasal verbs** verhalten sich jedoch anders, denn sie können nicht getrennt werden:

You can look up **the words** / look **the words** up	in a dictionary.
You can look **them** up	in a dictionary.
Please look after **my guinea pigs**.	Please look after **them**.

Einige Verben ähneln sich äußerlich, wobei aber eines intransitiv (= ohne Objekt) und das andere transitiv (= mit Objekt) verwendet wird.

Lucy fell off her bike.	*... fiel vom Fahrrad.*
Dad felled the old cherry tree yesterday.	*... fällte gestern den alten Kirschbaum ...*

Manche Verben haben zwei Objekte, ein direktes Objekt (meist eine Sache) und ein indirektes Objekt (meist eine Person/Personen). Es gibt daher zwei Möglichkeiten der Satzstellung (s. Bsp.).

	indirektes Obj.	**direktes Objekt**	**to + indirektes Objekt**
Mrs Doyle gave	the taxi driver	a ten-pound note.	
Mrs Doyle gave		a ten-pound note	**to** the taxi driver.

Bei Verben wie **explain** oder **introduce** steht das indirekte Objekt (= Personenobjekt) immer mit **to** nach dem direkten Objekt. Achtung: An **tell** wird das Personenobjekt direkt angeschlossen, an **say** wird es mit **to** angeschlossen.

She didn't tell **us** anything about her job.
She didn't say anything **to us** about her job.

May I introduce my colleague **to you**?

Bei manchen Verben steht das direkte Objekt mit einer Ergänzung. Das kann ein Substantiv oder Adjektiv mit oder ohne Präposition davor sein.

We thought him **intelligent**.

She has always looked upon her dad **as a hero**.

★ **1.** Alle Sätze enthalten ein **phrasal verb**. Markieren Sie die Antwort, die jeweils zum Bild passt.

a) 

- ☐ A It grows up.
- ☐ B It makes up.
- ☐ C It takes off.

b) 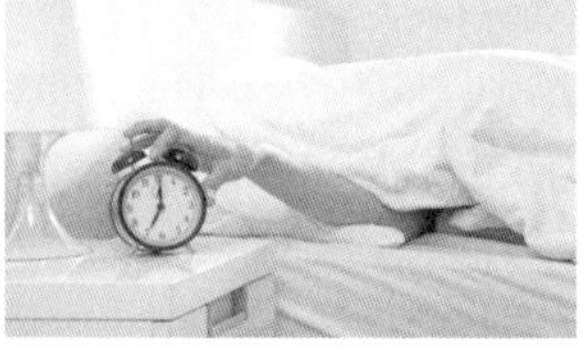

- ☐ A He looks it up.
- ☐ B He gets up early.
- ☐ C He comes along.

c) 

- ☐ A They look up a word.
- ☐ B They get up.
- ☐ C They pick up a book.

d) 

- ☐ A She is going away.
- ☐ B She is putting it on.
- ☐ C She is calling her friend up.

e) 

- ☐ A She came along.
- ☐ B Her boyfriend stood her up.
- ☐ C She rang up her friend.

★ **2.** Vervollständigen Sie den Satz, indem Sie die richtige Präposition auswählen.

a) I ran **into/at/down/for** an old friend of mine.

b) He couldn't do **without/for/across/after** his wife.

c) The boy called **at/for/in/to** help because he was drowning.

★★ **3.** Diese Verben ähneln sich, werden aber unterschiedlich verwendet. Setzen Sie sie an der jeweils richtigen Stelle ein.

a) What's happened? – I've ______________ off the tree. – Haven't you ______________ it yet? (fell, fall)

b) The chairman ______________ down and asked whether we had ______________ the timescale for the takeover. (sit, set)

c) We have to ______________ the table while mum does the cooking. After dinner we do the dishes and she ______________ on the sofa reading the paper. (lie, lay)

d) John's best man ______________ to give his speech. At the end, he ______________ his glass and wished the happy couple a safe journey to the Maldives. (raise, rise)

★★ **4.** Ersetzen Sie das Objekt (unterstrichen) durch ein Pronomen. Müssen Sie dann die Verbindung von **phrasal verb** und Präposition/Adverb trennen oder nicht?

Hier zwei Beispiele: You can **look up** <u>the words</u>. → You can **look** <u>them</u> **up**.
We **stand up** for <u>our rights</u>. → We **stand up** for <u>them</u>.

a) They cut off <u>our phone</u>. ______________

b) I'm counting on <u>your help</u>. ______________

c) Don't bring up <u>that topic</u> with her. ______________

d) Sarah didn't ask out <u>the neighbour</u>. ______________

e) My sister looks up to <u>our dad</u>. ______________

f) Clean up <u>this mess</u> before leaving. ______________

g) Jack relied on <u>his wife</u>. ______________

h) I came across <u>those old clothes</u> today. ______________

i) Look at <u>these beautiful pictures</u>! ______________

j) Liz took up <u>her new hobby</u> in June. ______________

★★ **5. Wie lautet die richtige Reihenfolge der beiden Objekte in diesen Sätzen? Mehr Informationen zu Bildung und Verwendung des Verbs bring.**

» PONS Verbtabellen Plus Englisch S. 46–47

a) Lucy / me / a cake / brought / for my birthday /.

---

b) The assistant / Mia / lots of pretty shirts / showed /.

---

c) The professor / to the students / the meaning of the poem / explained /.

---

d) Did / to you / say / about the new neighbours / anything / he /?

★★★ **6. Einigen englischen Verben folgt ein Objekt mit Ergänzung. Übersetzen Sie.**

a) Er machte sie sehr glücklich.

---

b) Ich finde das Buch über 1913 interessant.

---

c) Ich habe unsere Beziehung immer für natürlich gehalten.

---

d) Der Club wählte Carter zum Vorsitzenden.

---

e) Er betrachtete seine Wahl als selbstverständlich.

★★★ **7.** Einige **phrasal verbs** werden oft mit bestimmten Präpositionen benutzt, so dass auf das Verb gleich zwei Präpositionen folgen. Können Sie jeweils die richtige Kombination ergänzen?

a) He managed to get *out of* the burning house.

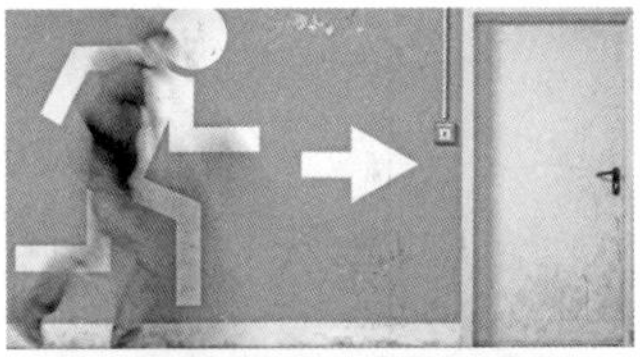

b) He couldn't keep ________________ his older brother.

c) You should watch ________________ dangerous animals.

d) We ran ________________ water in the middle of the desert.

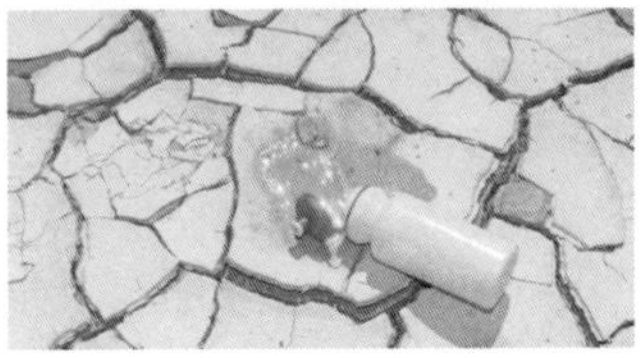

e) I hate him because he always

looks ________________ me.

f) We are really looking ________________ seeing you.

g) We should do ________________ some of the old plans.

22 GEBRAUCH DES PASSIVS

Man verwendet das Passiv, wenn man eine Handlung in den Vordergrund stellen will und weniger die handelnde(n) Person(en), z. B. wenn sie entweder nicht mehr oder noch nicht bekannt oder gar nicht wichtig ist (sind). Soll(en) sie doch genannt werden, so geschieht das mit Hilfe des **by-agent**.

Das Passiv wird im Englischen häufig in Zeitungsberichten, historischen Texten, Erklärungen und technischen Berichten sowie Geboten und Anweisungen verwendet. Der Gebrauch der Zeiten erfolgt nach denselben Prinzipien wie im Aktiv, jedoch sind **progressive**-Zeiten nur im **present** und **past tense** üblich.

The stolen car was found under a bridge by the police.
The fire doors must be kept free at all times.
The stadium on the hill is being enlarged at the moment.
When I drove past yesterday, additional spotlights were being installed.

Geht es um ungewollte oder unerwartete Ereignisse, kann umgangssprachlich auch das **get-passive** (» Kapitel 7: Passiv, S. 28) verwendet werden.

Phrasal verbs (» Kapitel 21: Verben und Ergänzungen, S. 97) werden im Passivsatz nicht getrennt:

Aktiv: The babysitter was looking after the children.
Passiv: The children were being looked after by the babysitter.

Hat das Verb **zwei Objekte**, gibt es zwei mögliche Passivsätze:

Aktiv: She gave the children some biscuits.
Passiv 1: The children were given some biscuits.
Passiv 2: Some biscuits were given **to** the children.

Werden Passivformen von **Verben des Sagens und Meinens** verwendet, steht danach oft eine Infinitivkonstruktion. Man kann solche Sätze mit einem *dass*-Satz übersetzen (s. Aktivsatz) oder mit Wendungen wie *soll(en) vermutlich/angeblich* ...

Aktiv: People say that swimming is the healthiest of all sports.
Passiv: Swimming is said to be the healthiest of all sports.

Das Passiv kann im **present simple** und **past simple** nicht nur einen Vorgang, sondern auch einen Zustand beschreiben. Im Deutschen verwendet man für das Zustandspassiv ein anderes Hilfsverb (sein) als für das Vorgangspassiv (werden).

Mum, I need the key – the garage is locked.	... *ist abgeschlossen.*
The doors are locked automatically at 8 o'clock.	... *werden abgeschlossen ...*

★ **1.** Das passive wird besonders für bestimmte Arten von Texten verwendet. Ordnen Sie die Beschreibungen den Sätzen unten richtig zu.

a) techn. Beschreibung ★ **b)** Zeitungsbericht ★ **c)** Anweisung ★ **d)** historischer Text

___ A According to the fire brigade, 22 houses were damaged during the storm.

___ B The dustbins must be put out every Wednesday.

___ C The pharaoh was buried in the year 1324 B.C.

___ D Plastic is made from oil.

★ **2.** Vervollständigen Sie diese Sätze mit der richtigen Verbform im **passive**. Achten Sie dabei auf Zeitangaben.

a) Yesterday, I **was/have been** told two important secrets by two different people!

b) As I came in, he **was/was being** asked about the whole thing. Then everything went quiet!

c) Do you know when they **are going to be awarded/are going to award** the prize?

d) If they found out, **will you be/would you be** disqualified from the competition?

e) I **have been/have been being** bullied for two years now and I'm sick of it!

★★ **3.** Bei welchen der folgenden Passiv-Sätze könnte es sich sowohl um einen Vorgang als auch einen Zustand handeln? Kreuzen Sie sie an.

a) ☐ The doors are locked at 8:00.

b) ☐ The sandwiches will be made when we arrive.

c) ☐ Our documentary is being shown at a film festival!

d) ☐ Be careful with that vase: it might be smashed.

e) ☐ She was given lots of presents.

★★ **4.** Wandeln Sie die folgenden Aktiv-Sätze ins **passive** um. In manchen Fällen benötigen Sie den **by-agent**, in anderen nicht.

a) Phil Collins has finally released a new album.

____

b) Someone might see you!

____

c) They are refitting the school cafeteria this term.

____

d) The British government will make the news public as soon as possible.

____

e) They founded the sailing club 40 years ago.

____

★★ **5.** Ergänzen Sie die Lücke mit dem passenden Verb. Achten Sie darauf, in welcher Zeitform der andere Satzteil geschrieben ist.

a) If I go, then you two ______________ left alone all night.

b) He says that, if you go, you ______________ awarded a prize!

c) If you ______________ contacted by the police, would you tell them anything about it?

d) If you were asked to participate in a survey, ______________ you?

e) ______________ you be told about it when it happens?

f) If you had a million pounds, you ______________ asked for money more often!

g) If you have your party two weeks after your birthday, when ______________ your presents be given to you?

★★ **6.** Wie muss hier das Verb im **passive** jeweils übersetzt werden?

a) There's no draught – the windows are closed. __________

b) The shutters are closed automatically at dusk. __________

c) The burglar was caught on the run by the police. __________

d) The car was repaired when I arrived at the garage. __________

★★ **7.** Können Sie diese Passivsätze wieder richtig zusammensetzen?

a) The children / after / looked / were / by our parents.

____

b) Last week / our road / into / two houses / broken / in / were /.

____

c) Cookies / were / to / given / the children / only /.

____

★★★ **8.** Übertragen Sie diese Sätze mit einer Passivkonstruktion ins Englische.

a) *Vitamine sollen angeblich gut für uns sein.*

____

b) *Man sagt, dass er den Preis unverdient erhalten hat.*

____

c) *Es heißt, dass die Epidemie in Westafrika begonnen hat.*

____

d) *Man nimmt an, dass sie in den Prüfungen mogelt.*

____

23 GEBRAUCH DES INFINITIVS

GEBRAUCH DES INFINITIVS MIT UND OHNE TO

» Übung 1–7

Der Infinitiv.

mit **to** steht:

- nach vielen Vollverben wie **want** (+ Objekt), z. B. nach Verben, die Wunsch oder Absicht ausdrücken (+ Objekt);
- nach Verben, die Aufforderung, Rat oder Warnung ausdrücken + Objekt;
- nach **the first/last/only one** und Superlativen
- nach Fragewörtern wie **what, where** etc. (verkürzt einen Nebensatz)

Jane wants (Dad/him) to help me.
She told you to leave the window open.
The Vikings were the first to discover North America.
I've no idea where to find the main road.

ohne **to** steht:

- nach den meisten modalen Hilfsverben sowie **will/would**;
- nach Verben des Wahrnehmens u. Beobachtens wie **see, hear** etc.;
- nach **make/have** und **let** + Objekt;
- nach **I'd rather/I'd better**
- in Fragen mit **why** (drückt aus, dass etw. unnötig/sinnlos ist) bzw. **why not** (für informelle Vorschläge)

Mike can help, too.
I've seen our cat play with a dog!
Mom let them stay for dinner.
I'd rather help you but I'd better go.
Why ask Jim? He won't come.

Außerdem kann der Infinitiv mit **to** Nebensätze ersetzen, z. B. des Zwecks, Ortes, der Zeit und Relativsätze sowie Nebensätze mit Fragewort (s.o.). Zur Verkürzung von Nebensätzen mit Partizipien » Kapitel 25: Gebrauch von Partizipien S. 116

She went to the market so that she could compare prices. >> ... to compare prices.
I offered Tim a book which he could read. >> ... to read.

Zur Bildung des Infinitivs und seinen Formen » Infinitiv, Partizipien und Gerund S. 20

INFINITIV ODER ING-FORM

» Übung 8–10

Einige Verben können sowohl den Infinitiv als auch die **ing**-Form (**gerund**) nach sich ziehen, **ohne** dass sich die Bedeutung des Satzes ändert. Die wichtigsten lauten: **love, like, hate , begin, continue, intend, prefer, start**.

My husband prefers working on his computer. *... bevorzugt die Arbeit ...*
I prefer to work in the garden. *... bevorzuge die Arbeit ...*

Bei manchen Verben ergibt sich aber eine **Bedeutungsänderung**, je nachdem, ob der Infinitiv oder die **ing**-Form folgt. Die wichtigsten lauten: **stop, forget, remember, regret, mean, try.**

She stopped reading. *Sie hörte auf zu lesen.*
She stopped to read the sign. *Sie hörte auf/hielt an, um das Schild zu lesen.*

Gebrauch des Infinitivs mit und ohne *to*

★ **1.** Ordnen Sie die Satzenden den Satzanfängen zu.

a) It was so embarrassing	___	A to hurt you.
b) They had a wild party, but afterwards they didn't know what	___	B to ask dad for some money.
c) I'm really sorry, I didn't mean	___	C to do with the broken bottles.
d) I don't have any shoes so I wanted	___	D to have a dignified death.
e) Our car is quite old, we plan	___	E to go shopping this afternoon.
f) You should respect a person's wish	___	F to get the best view of the area.
g) Mum asked us not	___	G to buy a new one next year.
h) We went right up to the top of the hill	___	H to join the party.
i) Sam was the last one	___	I to be back late.

★ **2.** Kreuzen Sie die korrekte Antwort auf die jeweilige Frage an.

a) Will Sam be home on time?
- ☐ A He promised to arrive not late.
- ☐ B He promised not to arrive late.
- ☐ C He didn't promise to be late.

b) May I speak to the doctor?
- ☐ A The doctor is not to be disturbed.
- ☐ B The doctor is to be not disturbed.
- ☐ C The doctor doesn't be disturbed.

c) Sam was late. Did he apologize?
- ☐ A Yes, he wasn't sorry to have phoned.
- ☐ B Yes, he was sorry to haven't phoned.
- ☐ C Yes, he was sorry not to have phoned.

d) Has Jack told you to fix the gate?
- ☐ A No, he has told me to fix it not.
- ☐ B No, he hasn't told me to fix it.
- ☐ C No, he hasn't told me to not fix it.

★ **3.** Nach welchen Verben oder Ausdrücken steht der Infinitiv ohne **to**, und nach welchen steht er mit **to**? Ordnen Sie die Satzanfänge in die Spalten ein.

» Gebrauch von Partizipien, S. 116, Übung 5

You may ... * The fireman warned us ... * Mr Butcher made me ... * She saw him ... * I don't know what ... * The doctor advised him ... * She would never ... * My parents let me ... You told her ... * Mary would like ... * Grandma wants ... * This is too much for me ... Did you hear them ... ? * Tom will be the first one ...

Infinitiv ohne **to**	Infinitiv mit **to**
______________________	______________________
______________________	______________________
______________________	______________________
______________________	______________________
______________________	______________________
______________________	______________________
______________________	______________________
______________________	______________________

★★ **4.** **Sie schreiben ihrer Brieffreundin in den USA. Füllen Sie die Lücken mit den jeweils passenden Verbkonstruktionen aus der Box in der richtigen Zeitform.**

happen to * be likely to * appear to * not seem to

Dear Jane,

I **(a)** ______________ meet my old teacher from primary school yesterday. When she asked me about my plans for university, I told her I'm still not sure what to do. Can you believe it? I **(b)** ______________ be able to make a decision, though I **(c)** ______________ get good marks for my final exams. I **(d)** ______________ need some advice ...

Best, Patrick,

★★ **5.** Bringen Sie die Satzteile in die richtige Reihenfolge. Achten Sie dabei auf die Stellung des Objekts.

a) leave / I / don't / want / to / you /.

____

b) the spectators / on / wanted / The athletes / to / them / cheer /.

____

c) step / him / asked / to / aside / Oliver /.

____

d) to / do / a / big / need / him / I / favour / me /.

____

e) her / with / him / Harry / expected / to / on / date / a / go /.

____

f) didn't / truth / to / the / him / I / tell / me / expect /.

____

★★ **6.** Anstelle verschiedener Nebensätze können auch Infinitivkonstruktionen stehen. Ersetzen Sie die Nebensätze (unterstrichen) entsprechend.

a) Could you tell me <u>where I can find a cash machine</u>?

____

b) We were given a list of books <u>which we should buy for the new school year</u>.

____

c) We chose seats right in front of the screen <u>so that we would get the best view</u>.

____

★★★ **7.** Folgende Sätze benötigen im Englischen besondere Infinitivformen (mit und ohne **to**)! Übersetzen Sie. Einmal sind zwei (ähnliche) Lösungen möglich.

a) *Wie immer ist vor Weihnachten starker Verkehr zu erwarten.*

____

b) *Jenna hat gerade einige Fotos gepostet. Sie scheint ihre Reise nach Italien zu genießen.*

____

c) *Es ist nichts zu essen mehr da. Du hättest eher kommen sollen.*

____

d) *Alex muss den Zug verpasst haben.*

____

e) *Sie entschied sich, ihn schließlich doch nicht zu fragen.*

____

Infinitiv oder ing-Form

★ **8.** Ob man den Infinitiv oder eine **ing**-Form verwendet, macht manchmal einen entscheidenden Unterschied. Welcher Satz gehört zu welcher Übersetzung?

a) I am used to Ian arriving late.
b) I would like to go out.
c) I like going out.
d) I stopped hitting him.
e) Ian used to arrive late.
f) I stopped to hit him.

___ A Ich habe aufgehört, ihn zu schlagen.
___ B Früher ist Ian zu spät gekommen.
___ C Ich möchte gerne ausgehen.
___ D Ich gehe gerne aus.
___ E Ich hielt an, um ihn zu schlagen.
___ F Ich bin es gewohnt, dass Ian zu spät kommt.

★★ **9.** Nach welchen Verben muss ein Infinitiv stehen, nach welchen eine **ing**-Form und nach welchen ist beides möglich (wenngleich teilweise mit unterschiedlicher Bedeutung)?

to look forward to * to mean * to stop * to be sorry * to ask * to want * to try * to insist on to like * to enjoy * to mind * to be afraid of

Infinitiv	**-ing**-Form	Infinitiv oder **-ing**-Form
______	______	______
______	______	______
______	______	______
______	______	______
______	______	______
______	______	______

★★★ **10.** Tragen Sie das in Klammern angegebene Verb entweder als Infinitiv oder als **ing**-Form ein.

a) He used to ______ (get) on my nerves when he was younger.

b) Megan was prepared to ______ (sacrifice) her happiness.

c) We went on to ______ (discuss) more important topics.

d) I am looking forward to ______ (meet) you.

e) Grace is used to ______ (clean) the house.

f) I can't understand them ______ (want) to live in Switzerland.

g) I object to people ______ (smoke) in my car.

h) I told the girls to come to the table, but they just went on ______ (play).

i) It's no use ______ (complain) about the price of fuel.

24 GEBRAUCH DES GERUND

Das **gerund** kann im Satz z. B. als Subjekt oder auch als Objekt erscheinen. Als Objekt steht es oft nach Verben der Vorliebe oder Abneigung.

Zur Bildung des **gerund** » Kapitel 4: Infinitiv, Partizipien und Gerund S. 20. Zur **-ing**-Form als **present participle** » Kapitel 25: Gebrauch von Partizipien S. 116.

Riding is her hobby.	*Reiten ist ihr Hobby.*
Writing reports is exhausting.	*Das Schreiben von Berichten ist anstrengend.*
She **loves** riding.	*Sie liebt das Reiten./ Sie liebt es, zu reiten.*
I **hate** writing reports.	*Ich hasse es, Berichte zu schreiben./ Ich hasse das Schreiben von Berichten/ Berichteschreiben.*

Steht ein Substantiv (z. B. ein Name) oder ein Pronomen in der Objektform **(me, her, them)** vor dem **gerund** in der Objektposition, so bezieht sich das **gerund** dann auf dieses Sinnsubjekt statt auf das eigentliche Subjekt im Satz:

Mum doesn't like watching horror films.	*Mama schaut sich nicht gerne Horrorfilme an.*
Mum doesn't like **us** watching horror films.	*Mama hat es nicht gern, dass wir Horrorfilme anschauen.*

Das **gerund** darf nicht mit den **progressive**-Formen verwechselt werden! Eine **progressive**-Form steht immer zusammen mit Hilfsverb(en):

Writing christmas cards is boring me. *Weihnachtskarten zu schreiben langweilt mich.*

Ein **gerund** steht auch

• nach bestimmten Verben mit Präposition, z. B. **rely on, think about/of, talk about/of, look forward to, succeed in, insist on** usw.	He always **insists on** being right. I **look forward to** seeing you.
• nach verbalen Ausdrücken mit Präposition, z. B. **be afraid of, be used to, be interested in**	She **is afraid of** touching spiders.
• nach bestimmten Substantiven mit Präposition **danger of, difficulty in, way of, idea of**	Many species are in **danger of** becoming extinct.
• und einigen anderen Ausdrücken wie z. B. **It's worth ..., It's no use ..., It's no good ... Thank you for ... ., How/What about ... ? Would you mind ... ?, without** usw.	**It's worth** reading the paper. **Thank you for** helping me. They just came in **without** knocking.

sowie nach einigen Verben, nach denen auch der Infinitiv stehen kann. Vorsicht: Manche Verben ändern ihre Bedeutung, je nachdem, ob ein Infinitiv oder ein **gerund** folgt. » Kapitel 23: Gebrauch des Infinitivs: Infinitiv oder ing-Form S. 106

★ **1.** Welche der Sätze enthalten ein **gerund**, welche eine andere Art **ing**-Form?

	gerund ja	nein
a) Clare likes riding very much.	☐	☐
b) She is going to help at her aunt's riding school all summer.	☐	☐
c) She learns fascinating things at her aunt's school.	☐	☐
d) Grooming the horses is fun, Clare thinks.	☐	☐
e) Clare's other favourite occupation is playing with the cats.	☐	☐
f) They are watching her while she is working in the stable.	☐	☐
g) Afterwards Clare strokes them until they're purring.	☐	☐

★ **2.** Bringen Sie die durcheinandergeratenen Satzteile in die richtige Reihenfolge und entscheiden Sie, ob das **gerund** jeweils Subjekt (S) oder Objekt (O) ist.

	S	O
a) can be / unknown restaurants / eating / in / disappointing /.	☐	☐
b) of / dancing / some friends / love / mine / the tango /.	☐	☐
c) with / can be / one's husband / shopping / for clothes / a challenge /.	☐	☐
d) sailing / I / enjoy /.	☐	☐
e) rather stressful / dozens of / having to write / christmas cards / is /.	☐	☐

★ **3.** Das **gerund** steht auch nach bestimmten Verben, verbalen Ausdrücken und Substantiven mit Präposition. Welche Präposition gehört zu welchem Begriff? Zweimal gibt es zwei richtige Lösungen.

about ⋆ in ⋆ of ⋆ in ⋆ about ⋆ of ⋆ about ⋆ about ⋆ of ⋆ on ⋆ to ⋆ of ⋆ on ⋆ in
of ⋆ of ⋆ of ⋆ at ⋆ of ⋆ about

a) think ________ **b)** succeed ________ **c)** dream ________

d) worry ________ **e)** insist ________ **f)** complain ________

g) rely ________ **h)** talk ________ **i)** look forward ________

j) danger ________ **k)** idea ________ **l)** be good/bad ________

m) way ________ **n)** be proud ________ **o)** be interested ________

p) difficulty ________ **q)** be crazy ________ **r)** be ashamed ________

★★ **4.** Übersetzen Sie die Sätze ins Englische und benutzen Sie dabei ein **gerund**.

a) *Segeln ist entspannend.*

____

b) *Balletttanzen ist das größte Hobby unserer Tochter.*

____

c) *Ich interessiere mich für das Erlernen eines Instruments.*

____

d) *Mein Mann zieht es vor, morgens Kaffee zu trinken.*

____

e) *Ich liebe es, abends zu lesen.*

____

★★★ **5. Bilden Sie die korrekte Form des Verbs und des jeweiligen Sinnsubjekts.**

a) Dad wants ____________ (Chris/go) to a dog school with his dog.

b) I didn't expect ____________ (he/become) so angry.

c) He's tired of ____________ (you/bark) all day long, Wolfie.

★★★ **6. Nach einigen Verben kann ein gerund oder ein infinitive stehen, manchmal entsteht aber ein Bedeutungsunterschied. Kreuzen Sie an, welche Sätze je nach Verbform ihre Bedeutung ändern.** (» Kapitel 23: Gebrauch des Infinitivs, S. 106)

a) I stopped **working/to work** when my boss came in. ☐

b) Harry likes **sailing/to sail** in the Caribbean. ☐

c) Mum remembered **bringing/to bring** your magazine. ☐

d) Tom continues **looking/to look** for the perfect job. ☐

★★★ **7. Nach welchen dieser teilweise sehr ähnlichen Ausdrücke steht das gerund, nach welchen der infinitive?** (» Kapitel 23: Gebrauch des Infinitivs, S. 106)

a) It's no good ____________ (feed) a dog three times a day.

b) It's important ____________ (train) your dog.

c) It's not good ____________ (keep) a dog indoors for too long.

d) There's no ____________ (know) how it might react.

e) It's a pity for all those animals not ____________ (be) cared for properly.

f) It's no use ____________ (complain) about the weather.

g) It's not very sensible ____________ (hang) the washing out in the rain.

h) It's worth ____________ (give) the idea a try.

i) It's unusual for her ____________ (refuse) to listen.

25 GEBRAUCH VON PARTIZIPIEN

Das **present participle** und das **past participle** können als Adjektive benutzt werden, z. B. vor einem Substantiv oder als Verbergänzung. (» Kapitel 21: Verben und Ergänzungen S. 97; » Zur Bildung der Partizipien Kapitel 4: Infinitiv, Partizipien und Gerund S. 20)

The driver of the battered taxi remained sitting.
Der Fahrer des verbeulten Taxis blieb sitzen.

Das **present participle** nach Verben wie **see, hear, notice, feel, find, watch, observe** + Objekt drückt aus, dass der Ablauf eines Geschehens (oder eines Teils davon) beobachtet wird. Steht stattdessen der Infinitiv ohne **to**, bedeutet das, dass die ganze Handlung oder eine Handlungsfolge wahrgenommen wird.

» Kapitel 23: Gebrauch des Infinitivs S. 106

I **saw** them leaving the house.	*Ich sah, wie sie das Haus verließen.*
I **saw** them leave the house, get into their car and drive off.	*Ich sah sie das Haus verlassen, ins Auto einsteigen und wegfahren.*

Das **present participle** nach Verben wie **come, go, sit, stand, lie, remain** drückt zwei gleichzeitig ablaufende Handlungen aus. Steht das **past participle** nach **remain** oder **lie**, wird dadurch ein Ergebnis ausgedrückt.

They **stayed** talking long after the meeting was over.	*Sie blieben ... und redeten ...*
The Alps **lie** covered in snow.	*... liegen schneebedeckt da.*

Die Konstruktion **have** (und ugs. **get**) + Objekt + **past participle** drückt aus, dass eine Tätigkeit veranlasst wird. Achten Sie auf die richtige Stellung des Objekts, um eine Verwechslung mit dem **present perfect** zu vermeiden (s. Bsp.). Achtung: Die Verben **make/have** – *veranlassen, dass jemand etwas tut* – sowie **let** – *zulassen, dass jemand etwas tut* – *verhalten sich ähnlich* (» Kapitel 23: Gebrauch des Infinitivs S. 106).

He always **has** his car washed.	*Er lässt immer sein Auto waschen.*
But this time he has washed his car himself.	*... hat er es selbst gewaschen.*

Außerdem können die Partizipien Nebensätze (der Zeit, des Orts, des Grundes ...) verkürzen, sowie auch Relativsätze und sogar Hauptsätze. Beachten Sie, dass solche Partizipialkonstruktionen fast immer förmlich wirken, außer bei Relativsätzen oder wenn sie mit **with** eingeleitet werden.

When we left the harbour, we saw a rainbow.	When leaving the harbour, ...
As she had been warned about mosquitoes, she decided to use a strong repellent.	Warned about mosquitoes, ...
We drove to a garden party. Our friends joined us.	... , our friends joining us.
Many of the people who live in this area are Greek.	... living in this area ...
It's been a busy day. The telephone's been ringing all the time.	It's been a busy day, with the telephone ringing all the time.

★ **1.** Das **present participle** und das **past participle** können als Adjektive benutzt werden. Finden Sie zu den Formen jeweils das passende Bild. Zur Bildung des **present** und **past participle** » Kapitel 4: Infinitiv, Partizipien und Gerund S. 20. Siehe auch » PONS Verbtabellen Plus Englisch S. 44–45 und 166–167 zur Bildung der Verbformen von **break** und **sleep**.

a) sleeping

b) smiling

___ A 

___ B 

c) forbidden

d) burning

___ C 

___ D 

e) dancing

f) walking

___ E 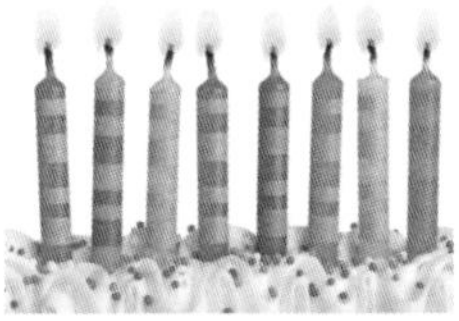

___ F 

g) freezing

h) married

___ G 

___ H 

i) annoyed

j) broken

___ I 

___ J 

★ **2.** Hier drückt das **present participle** den Ablauf eines Geschehens aus, das beobachtet wird/wurde. Können Sie die Sätze wieder richtig zusammensetzen?

a) The children / moving in / the new neighbours / watched /.

b) talking / old Mrs Miller / I / hear / on the telephone / always /.

c) Have / Mr Butcher / seen / trimming / you / the hedge?

d) Did / you / notice / circling / the police helicopter / yesterday /?

★ **3.** Mithilfe von Partizipien kann man gleichzeitig ablaufende Handlungen be-schreiben oder auch das Ergebnis einer abgeschlossenen Handlung. Übertragen Sie die Sätze ins Deutsche.
Zu einigen der Verben finden Sie weitere Informationen in » PONS Verbtabellen Plus Englisch S. 172–73 (stand), S. 186–87 (wait), S. 66–7 (come), S. 122–23 (lie).

a) We stood waiting outside the club for ages.

b) A cute dog came sniffing at me.

c) The logs are stacked behind the house.

d) At this temperature, the streets remain covered in snow.

★ **4.** Ordnen Sie die Sätze den passenden Bildern zu. Achten Sie dabei darauf, wie im Englischen mit der **ing**-Form ein Nebensatz gebildet werden kann.

A

B

C

D

E

F

____ **a)** After talking to him the whole night, she was disappointed that she didn't get his number.

____ **b)** Without showing any fear, he faced the bull.

____ **c)** Oscar was in the park reading books.

____ **d)** Having finally found the right present, she was ready to go to the party.

____ **e)** She can't work properly with all that noise going on.

____ **f)** Most of the things sold in this shop come from India.

★★ **5.** Mit dem Verb **have** (und **get** in der Umgangssprache) in Verbindung mit einem **past participle** kann man ausdrücken, dass man etwas machen lässt. Vervollständigen Sie die Sätze richtig mit Hilfe der Vorgaben. Vorsicht: es haben sich einige ähnliche Verben eingeschlichen!

» Kapitel 23: Gebrauch des Infinitivs S. 106

a) He usually ______________ (have/cut/his hair) once a month.

b) Mum always ______________ (make/carry out/Dad) the rubbish.

c) Please ______________ (let/keep/me) the kitten!

d) Our bikes are really run-down. Let's ______________ (get/repair/them).

e) Yesterday Grandma ______________ (have/deliver/everything) she needs for her christmas cookies.

★★★ **6.** Verschiedene Satzarten können mit einem Partizip verkürzt werden. Verkürzen Sie die markierten Satzteile und schreiben Sie die Sätze entsprechend um.

a) The girl <u>who is waiting at the bus stop</u> is one of my daughter's friends.

____

b) <u>When we looked down from the plane</u>, we saw the lights of the city below.

____

c) <u>While I was staying in London</u>, I met one of my old friends from university.

____

d) The guide led the way to the bus. <u>The tourists followed with their souvenirs</u>.

____

e) <u>Winter is coming fast</u>, so Chris has stopped cycling to work.

With ____

TEIL 1: VERBFORMEN ÜBEN

1. Voll- und Hilfsverben

1.

a) teaches, **b)** knows, **c)** Are, **d)** Do, **e)** don't, **f)** has

2.

teaches, knows, Are, has

3.

a) said, **b)** arrived, **c)** took, **d)** saw, went
e) didn't meet, **f)** Did (we) enjoy

4.

a) wasn't, **b)** weren't, **c)** didn't work, **d)** hadn't, **e)** didn't do

5.

	to be	**to do**	**to have**
I	am not	do	have
You	aren't	do	have
he/she/it	isn't	does	has
We	aren't	do	have
you	aren't	do	have
they	aren't	do	have

6.

a) C, **b)** B, **c)** B, **d)** A

7.

a) do, **b)** would, **c)** Do, **d)** How do you do?, **e)** have, **f)** aren't, **g)** Have, **h)** –

8.

a), **c)** und **d)**: **do**, **e)** und **g)**: **have**, **f)**: aren't (von *to be*)

9.

a) C, **b)** B, **c)** A, **d)** C, **e)** C

10.

a) turning, **b)** played, **c)** dream, **d)** go, **e)** going, **f)** had an zweiter Stelle, **g)** going, **h)** fell, **i)** have got, **j)** have
past: **b)**, **e)**, **f)**, **h)**; present: **a)**, **g)**, **i)**, **j)**;
future: **c)**, **d)**

11.

a) I'll have gone, **b)** You won't have seen, **c)** It'll have grown, **d)** She'll have forgiven, **e)** They won't have tried, **f)** We'll have understood, **g)** He won't have had

12.

a) Who helps me? **b)** Who doesn't like cats? **c)** Who can call Andrew? **d)** Who do you marry? **e)** Who will Andrew see? **f)** What does Emma want? **g)** Who would like some tea? **h)** What do you know?

13.

a) She hasn't been trying to help me. **b)** Have you seen him smoking? **c)** The catamaran was moving very fast. **d)** They'd been looking really ill. **e)** I wouldn't have gone there.

2. Modalverben

1.

must, may, should, need, can, shall, will, ought to

2.

a) must; **b)** Can; **c)** needs; **d)** can't; **e)** must; **f)** needn't

3.

a) she won't be able to; **b)** he may not, veraltet auch: mayn't; **c)** they won't be allowed to; **d)** they mustn't; **e)** it wouldn't; **f)** we hadn't had to; **g)** you shouldn't veraltet auch: you oughtn't

4.

a) B, D; **b)** C, E; **c)** F; **d)** A

5.

(von links nach rechts und von oben nach unten) would want, will want; will be able to, going to be able to; would have to, going to have to

6.

a) would have wanted; **b)** would not have been able to achieve; **c)** would have had to find/to have found; **d)** would have been allowed to do; **e)** would you have done

Lösungen

3. Regelmäßige, unregelmäßige und reflexive Verben

1.

a) B; **b)** A; **c)** C

2.

(jeweils von oben nach unten)
to be: are, is, are, are;
to go: go, goes, go;
to see: see, sees, see

3.

-s: says, buys, enjoys, plays, pays;
-ies: carries, tries, cries, studies, hurries

4.

a) herself; **b)** myself; **c)** ---; **d)** himself;
e) ---; **f)** ourselves; **g)** themselves;
h) ---; **i)** ---; **j)** ---; **k)** themselves

5.

past simple: blew, lay, beat;
past simple/participle: swung, paid, left, brought;
participle: run, risen, sawn, stolen

6.

a) cut; **b)** behave; **c)** help

7.

a) herself; **b)** myself; **c)** yourself;
d) each other; **e)** myself; **f)** each other;
g) each other

8.

a) backslid; **b)** resent; **c)** persuaded;
d) populated; **e)** undercut; **f)** misled;
g) reset; **h)** dived

9.

regular: reached, tended, turned, looked;
regular/irregular: leant/leaned, learnt/learned, bet/betted, spelt/spelled;
irregular: quit, struck, wore, fought

4. Infinitiv, Partizipien und Gerund

1.

Infinitive: go, be, talk, make, rain;
present participles: doing, walking, having;
past participles: done, had

2.

leave > leaving; smile > smiling; put > putting; write > writing; run > running; lie > lying

3.

(von links nach rechts und von oben nach unten:) answer, answered; sitting, sat; love, loving; cut, cutting; seeing, seen; dying, died; making, made

4.

a) understood (PA); **b)** discussing (PR);
c) inviting (PR); **d)** forgotten (PA)

5.

a) A (beaten), **b)** B (sat), **c)** D (said)

6.

a) doing, **b)** found, **c)** Having been confined, **d)** revising, **e)** had, **f)** be working, **g)** Having eaten, **h)** enjoyed

5. Leicht verwechselbare Verben

1.

a) rises, **b)** see, **c)** find, **d)** lie, **e)** break, **f)** lays

2.

saw, lay, found

3.

(von links nach rechts und von oben nach unten:) find, found; found, founded, founded; rise, rose; raise, raised, raised; see, seen; saw, sawn

4.

a) B, **b)** A

5.

a) find, **b)** risen, **c)** sawing, **d)** struck, **e)** saw, **f)** lay back, **g)** found

6.

a) D; **b)** C; **c)** A; **d)** F; **e)** B; **f)** E

6. Imperativ

1.

a) turn off, **b)** stop, **c)** Don't drive, **d)** Mind, **e)** Be

2.

a) Don't try to do this at home. **b)** Let's have our picnic here. **c)** Never forget to lock your door.

3.

a) Let's go to the cinema. **b)** Let's not visit Aunt Mary today. **c)** Let's go swimming instead.

7. Passiv

1.

Aktiv: a), b), e), g); **Passiv:** c), d), f), h)

2.

a) D, **b)** C, **c)** B, **d)** A

3.

a) had done, **b)** have seen, **c)** was going

4.

a) It is being repaired; **b)** The shirts are being made; **c)** We were being helped; **d)** I am being examined; **e)** My bike was being stolen

5.

a) He got badly hurt in the accident.
b) Your bike might get stolen outside.
c) Unfortunately we got bitten by mosquitoes at the picnic.

6.

Aktiv: b), c), f), g); **Passiv:** a), d), e), h)
Die Aktivformen lauten im Passiv: **b)** It was being lost, **c)** They have been being looked after, **f)** She had been offended, **g)** We are being left
Die Passivformen lauten im Aktiv: **a)** I have offered, **d)** They told, **e)** She had given, **h)** I was beating

7.

a) Many letters are written to the president. **b)** Our neighbour's cat is being rescued by firemen right now. **c)** Politicians are criticized for using abstract language. **d)** The cupcakes were eaten by the children. **e)** My car was taken to the garage yesterday. **f)** While my car was being repaired, I went by train.

8.

a) Are many letters written to the president?
b) Is our neighbour's cat being rescued by firemen right now? **c)** Politicians aren't criticized for using abstract language.
d) Were the cupcakes eaten by the children?
e) The cupcakes weren't eaten by the children. **f)** My car wasn't taken to the garage yesterday.

9.

a) was given, **b)** had already been awarded, **c)** has finally been released, **d)** is going to be performed, **e)** will not be made, **f)** is being refitted, **g)** must be kept, **h)** should have been replaced

10.

a) The match is won. **b)** The small island was discovered. **c)** The ball is thrown. **d)** The thief is caught. **e)** Our clothes were washed. **f)** A mistake was made. **g)** The eggs are being counted.

8. Konjunktiv

1.

a) B, C, D, **b)** A, B, C

2.

a) it wouldn't be, **b)** they wouldn't watch, **c)** we wouldn't do, **d)** you would'nt go, **e)** they would not be able, **f)** you wouldn't know, **g)** she wouldn't have, **h)** I wouldn't want

3.

a) she wouldn't leave, **b)** I wouldn't have thought, **c)** it wouldn't do, **d)** they would be seeing, **e)** he'd have had, **f)** you'd be having

4.

A, C, E, F, H

5.

a) Du könntest Oma fragen. Sie wüsste, was zu tun ist. **b)** Ich frage mich immer noch, ob ich diese Eintrittskarten hätte kaufen sollen.

6.

a) I would have apologized for provoking her. **b)** Why wouldn't he leave a message? **c)** You should have spoken to the boss first. **d)** I'm sure they would tell me the truth.

7.

von links nach rechts und von oben nach unten: would be able to, would be allowed to, would be supposed to; would have been able to, would have been allowed to, would have been supposed to

8.

a) could he, **b)** would she, **c)** should I, **d)** wouldn't you, **e)** would they

9. Bildung: Present tense und present perfect

Present tense

1.

write, eats, show, sees, likes, go, does, am, sleep, is, flies, are, teaches

2.

hope, see, know, taste, belong, sound, hate, forget, love, imagine, cost, understand

3.

a) begins, **b)** is, **c)** has, see, **d)** rings, is, **e)** ends

4.

a) A, **b)** B, **c)** B, **d)** C, **e)** B

5.

a) do you? **b)** aren't they? **c)** don't they? **d)** is it?, **e)** can she? **f)** mustn't we? **g)** doesn't it? **h)** isn't it?

6.

von links nach rechts und von oben nach unten: do, does, doesn't do, is doing, isn't doing; be, is, isn't, is being, isn't being; tries, doesn't try, is trying, isn't trying; take, takes, is taking, isn't taking

7.

a) Are the Millers enjoying their trip through Canada? **b)** Where are you going tonight? **c)** Is Dad watching a car race on TV again?

8.

a) What do you like? **b)** Are you just speaking to Matt? **c)** What is she looking for? **d)** Who says there are going on holiday tomorrow? **e)** When does their plane leave?

Present perfect

9.

a) I haven't gone, **b)** She hasn't been, **c)** We haven't seen, **d)** He hasn't done, **e)** They haven't eaten, **f)** It hasn't taken

10.

a) left, **b)** been, **c)** heard, **d)** has, **e)** finished, **f)** Have

11.

a) I haven't been going; **b)** They haven't been making; **c)** She hasn't been leaving; **d)** We haven't been choosing; **e)** He hasn't been informing; **f)** It hasn't been developing

12.

a) has been changing, **b)** have been growing, **c)** have been struggling, **d)** have been expanding, **e)** have been studying, **f)** have been using

13.

a) Has David left the money in an envelope? **b)** I have forgotten to pass on the message. **c)** Their teacher has not asked for the homework yet. **d)** You have written an exciting story. **e)** Has she seen the film already?

14.

a) hasn't she? **b)** has he? **c)** haven't they? **d)** hasn't he? **e)** have you? **f)** haven't I? **g)** have we?

15.

a) been, **b)** having, **c)** been, **d)** been, **e)** has, **f)** have, had, **g)** Have, have, **h)** have, **i)** been, have

10. Bildung: Past tense und past perfect

1.

a) B, **b)** D, **c)** B

2.

a) wasn't, **b)** couldn't, **c)** didn't go, **d)** weren't, **e)** didn't work, **f)** hadn't

3.

a) asked, **b)** advised, **c)** encouraged

4.

a) A; **b)** A; **c)** B; **d)** D

5.

a) were being, was being; **b)** were eating, was eating; **c)** were forgetting, was forgetting; **d)** were discussing, was discussing

6.

a) It wasn't being, **b)** He wasn't doing, **c)** We weren't eating, **d)** I wasn't being asked

7.

a) Yes, he was doing his homework. **b)** Yes, the dog was barking. **c)** Yes, they were eating sweets in the kitchen. **d)** Yes, she was crying. **e)** Yes, they were playing games.

8.

a) They had all had a slice of cake before I got one. **b)** Had you already heard the news before I told you? **c)** I had just come in when you gave me a call. **d)** We weren't hungry because we had just eaten lunch.

9.

a) It hadn't developed, **b)** They hadn't paid, **c)** We hadn't chosen, **d)** He hadn't informed

10.

a) Our children used to enjoy horror films. **b)** Did she use to work in insurance? **c)** He never used to be very ambitious.

11.

a) had been receiving, **b)** had been trying, **c)** had been rising, **d)** had been forecasting

12.

a) had left, **b)** managed, **c)** should take, **d)** had been

11. Bildung: Future tenses

1.

The plan for next week's class trip to London is as follows.
We will all meeting* → will all meet at the airport at 7.00 am for check-in at 8.00 am. If anyone goes to be late* → is going to be late (e.g. due to traffic), they need to call Mr. Thompson. We are due in London at 9.00 am and will spend the first day sightseeing. There wont* → won't be any time to check into the hotel until the evening, so everyone will needs* → will need to pack as little as possible. Mr. Thompson is going try* → is going to try and find a place to leave luggage, however, before next week.

2.

a) He isn't going to do, **b)** She isn't going to mind, **c)** I'm not going to like, **d)** We aren't going to be

3.

a) She will be eighteen in a few years. **b)** He is going to play football this afternoon. **c)** I will be at the station in ten minutes. **d)** Are you not going to come out? **e)** Will it not be more difficult? **f)** Isn't he going to finish it?

4.

a) Dad will go to the supermarket tomorrow. **b)** I will not/won't forget to pass on the message. **c)** Will you be at the party on Friday? **d)** She will give you the key when you arrive. **e)** Will he play in the match next week? **f)** Will they not/Won't they come on Sunday?

5.

a) D, **b)** B, **c)** C, **d)** A, **e)** D

6.

von links nach rechts und von oben nach unten: will go, is going to go, is going, will be going; will be, is going to be, is being, will be being; will have, is going to have, is having, will be having; will try, is going to try, is trying, will be trying

7.

future progressive: a), b), f), g)
future perfect: c), d), e), h)

8.

a) B, **b)** F, **c)** E, **d)** A, **e)** D, **f)** C

9.

a) I'll have gone, **b)** You won't have seen, **c)** It'll have grown, **d)** She'll have been forgiving, **e)** They won't have been trying, **f)** We'll have been understanding, **g)** He won't have been sleeping

10.

a) am/'m going, **b)** were going, **c)** wasn't going, **d)** was going, **e)** are going, **f)** were going, **g)** am not going, **h)** were going

11.

a) was meeting, **b)** were going to move in, **c)** Will ... be keeping, **d)** will have gone swimming, will have been working, **e)** would help

TEIL 2: VERBEN RICHTIG BENUTZEN

12. Present simple und progressive

1.

a) is, **b)** am, **c)** hope, **d)** can, **e)** don't, **f)** like, **g)** are, **h)** do

2.

simple: often, these days, regularly, usually, sometimes, always, never
progressive: now, at the moment, this season

3.

a) usually take out, **b)** am, **c)** is talking, **d)** are worrying

4.

a) live, **b)** is taking, **c)** is, **d)** needs, **e)** is showing

5.

a) usually wash; **b)** 'm washing ; **c)** don't eat; **d)** dislike; **e)** 's celebrating; **f)** arrives; **g)** 's doing .... think ... enjoys; **h)** takes care; **i)** belongs; cycles; **j)** takes; doesn't conclude

6.

a) I'm talking on the phone at the moment. **b)** Robbie and Ken are eating apples right now. **c)** Bob and Carl cook together quite often. **d)** Tara likes fresh salad – especially in the summer. **e)** Cindy can't take the call because she is driving. **f)** The boys don't want to come in although it's raining.

13. Present perfect simple und progressive

1.

a) been, **b)** doing, **c)** I've, **d)** moving, **e)** painting, **f)** have

2.

since: 2010, I was a child, 24th May, 3 o'clock, last year;
for: years, ages, two hours, a couple of months

3.

a) found, **b)** has grown, **c)** left, **d)** has read

4.

a) H, **b)** C, **c)** B, **d)** F, **e)** E, **f)** A, **g)** G, **h)** D

5.

a) did go, **b)** Have ... got, **c)** 's/has been, **d)** wrote, **e)** 've/have been working, **f)** 've/have been revising, **g)** 've/have decided, **h)** 've/have bought, **i)** 've/have asked, **j)** Have ... considered

6.

a) Have you been learning German for long? **b)** How often have you been to London? **c)** I've just been there on holiday. Now I am back again.

14. Past tense und past perfect

1.

a) B, **b)** D, **c)** A, **d)** C

2.

a) were having, **b)** ran, **c)** was thinking, **d)** knocked, **e)** brought, **f)** patted, **g)** was explaining, **h)** was having, **i)** proposed

3.

I know that: they are not here, she will be going as well, he has tried hard, it has improved a lot, things have changed, you can't make it; You said that: he had tried hard, things had changed, they weren't here, she would be going as well, it had improved a lot, you couldn't make it

4.

a), b), d), g), h)

5.

a) looking, **b)** asked, **c)** didn't, **d)** am, **e)** want, **f)** don't, **g)** said, **h)** promise, **i)** replied

6.

a) E, **b)** D, **c)** F, **d)** B, **e)** C, **f)** A

7.

a) Didn't she/you realise that she/you had never flown before? **b)** Daniel told me that you had been away on holiday all week. **c)** My cat had been scratching the sofa for hours when we got back. **d)** I had been chatting with her for half an hour by then. **e)** Have you been told that he is having trouble with the work? **f)** Craig heard that you weren't coming to the party.

8.

a) D, **b)** A, **c)** B, **d)** D

9.

a) went, **b)** was doing, **c)** had gone, **d)** was going, **e)** did, **f)** had been having

10.

a) had left, **b)** live, **c)** had managed, **d)** not to sign, **e)** would like, **f)** had been, **g)** to climb

11.

a) hadn't been **b)** had stolen, **c)** went, **d)** arrived, had lost, **e)** wanted, **f)** had travelled, loved, **g)** had paid, **h)** had seen

15. Future tenses

1.

a) Are, **b)** will, **c)** leaves, **d)** going, **e)** won't, **f)** will

2.

a) I'll go, **b)** They'll play, **c)** We won't, **d)** He'll do

3.

a) be, **b)** going, **c)** won't, **d)** to, **e)** be, **f)** are, **g)** Will, **h)** were

4.

a) D, **b)** C, **c)** B, **d)** F, **e)** A, **f)** E

5.

a) am going to finish, **b)** will go out, **c)** will find, **d)** was going to come, **e)** will have travelled, **f)** won't have done, **g)** won't worry, **h)** will have read

6.

a) C, **b)** B

7.

a) will have been looking, **b)** will have looked, **c)** will have to look, **d)** will look, **e)** will be looking, **f)** will have, **g)** would look

8.

a) F, **b)** C, **c)** G, **d)** E, **e)** D, **f)** H, **g)** B, **h)** A

9.

a) will have been looking, won't have found, **b)** will have been travelling, **c)** will probably have thought, **d)** will have happened, will have melted

10.

a) would, **b)** had **c)** forgotten, **d)** need, **e)** be, **f)** will **g)** able, **h)** going, **i)** have **j)** been **k)** travelling

11.

a) will have been learning, **b)** 'm going, **c)** will have travelled, **d)** will be raining, **e)** 'll just wait, **f)** won't have been waiting, **g)** 're playing

16. Gebrauch des Conditional

1.

a) B, höfliche Bitten, **b)** D, höfliche Fragen, **c)** A, Bedingungssätze (if-Sätze), **d)** C, höfliche Vorschläge oder Anregungen

2.

a) C, **b)** E, **c)** A, **d)** D, **e)** B

3.

a) wouldn't, **b)** Could, **c)** wouldn't, **d)** gave, **e)** Will, **f)** is, **g)** 'd

4.

a) went, **b)** do, **c)** going, **d)** sitting, **e)** could, **f)** sent, **g)** would, **h)** be, **i)** find, **j)** wouldn't

5.

a) could, **b)** will go, **c)** told, **d)** 'll meet, 'll all go, **e)** weren't, **f)** would you say, **g)** goes, **h)** were allowed to, **i)** had to

6.

a) be lying, **b)** have been lying, **c)** have said, **d)** be playing, **e)** have been waiting, **f)** wait

7.

a) A, **b)** C, **c)** A, **d)** B

8.

a) would buy, **b)** had, **c)** would lead, **d)** did, **e)** would go, **f)** ate, **g)** were, **h)** wouldn't know

9.

a) She would buy a car if she had the money. **b)** I would have lost the game if Daniel had played. **c)** I would have gone mad if it weren't for my lovely cat. **d)** If I had seen the rabbit in time, I would have braked.

10.

a) would have been, **b)** would have been lying, **c)** would have wanted, **d)** would have been able to go/could have gone, **e)** would have had to pull out/would have had to have pulled out, **f)** would still have been sitting

11.

a) D, wouldn't have happened, **b)** F, would have lost, **c)** B, hadn't bought, **d)** E, had studied, **e)** A, would have stayed, **f)** C, hadn't fallen

12.

a) would have wanted, **b)** would not have been able to achieve/could not have achieved, **c)** would have had to find/to have found, **d)** Would they have been allowed to go out...?, **e)** would have been supposed to eat/should have eaten

13.

a) save, **b)** were, **c)** keep, **d)** were, **e)** help, **f)** were, **g)** weren't, **h)** be, **i)** give, **j)** were

17. Stellung des Verbs im Satz

1.

a) Claire is painting. **b)** Claire is painting a picture for Tim. **c)** Benjamin doesn't live in Germany. **d)** Tom went to Dublin yesterday. **e)** Annette has never been to South Africa.

2.

a) ..., isn't she? **b)** ..., does he? **b)** ..., didn't he? **d)** ..., has she?

3.

a) So am I. **b)** So can I. **c)** ..., and so does Betty. **d)** Neither/Nor are Jill and Mike.

4.

a) Does Mary like camping? **b)** When would you like to go? **c)** Where have they been?

5.

a) barely, **b)** never, **c)** scarcely, **d)** hardly, **e)** nowhere, **f)** rarely, **g)** neither, **h)** seldom

6.

a) Hardly had she left the house when it started to rain. **b)** Never did I see such a crowd of people. **c)** Nowhere was the car key to be found although I looked everywhere.

18. Gebrauch der Modalverben

1.

a) B (Bereitschaft), **b)** D (Angebot), **c)** A (Rat/Ermahnung/Pflicht), **d)** E (Fähigkeit/Unfähigkeit), **e)** C (Verbot)

2.

a) D, **b)** C, **c)** A, **d)** B

3.

b) Yes, I would. /No, I wouldn't. **c)** Yes, I can. /No, I can't. **d)** Yes, you may. /No, you may not. **e)** Yes, she is. /No, she isn't. **f)** Yes, you must. /No, you needn't. **g)** Yes, I want to. / No, I don't want to. **h)** Yes, I would. /No, I wouldn't. **i)** Yes, you need to. /No, you needn't. **j)** Yes, they were. /No, they weren't. **k)** Yes, I did. /No, I didn't.

4.

a) can't, isn't able to; **b)** may, is allowed to; **c)** Will, Would; **d)** shouldn't, oughtn't to; **e)** mustn't, are not allowed to; **f)** must

5.

a) B, **b)** B, **c)** B, **d)** B, **e)** D, **f)** C

19. Gebrauch des Imperativs

1.

a) D, **b)** C, **c)** B, **d)** A

2.

Aufforderungen (a), Einladungen (b), Hinweise/Hinweisschilder (c), Verbote/ Verbotsschilder (d)

3.

a) In case of an emergency call 112. **b)** Sign here. **c)** Do sit down./Sit down, please. **d)** Let's not/Don't let's come back too late.

20. Leicht verwechselbare Verben und Verben in festen Wendungen

1.

a) B, **b)** A, **c)** B, **d)** B, **e)** A, **f)** B, **g)** A

2.

a) overtake, **b)** controlled, **c)** spends, **d)** oversee, **e)** complain, **f)** checked

3.

a) having; **b)** got (auch: received); **c)** get/have; **d)** have/get

4.

a) borrow, lend, **b)** bringing, take, **c)** wearing, carrying, **d)** listening, heard, **e)** remember, remind, **f)** risen, raised, **g)** said, told

5.

a) Frank macht sehr gern Bergwanderungen. **b)** Ich kann mich am Freitag leider nicht mit dir treffen. **c)** Wir trafen bei der Ausstellung zufällig die Scotts.

21. Verben und Ergänzungen

1.

a) C, **b)** B, **c)** A, **d)** C, **e)** B

2.

a) into, **b)** without, **c)** for

3.

a) fallen, felled; **b)** Sit, set; **c)** lay, lies; **d)** rose, raised

4.

a) They cut it off. **b)** I'm counting on it. **c)** Don't bring it up with her. **d)** Sarah didn't ask him out. **e)** My sister looks up to him. **f)** Clean it up before leaving. **g)** Jack relied on her. **h)** I came across them today. **i)** Look at them! **j)** Liz took it up in June.

5.

a) Lucy brought me a cake for my birthday. **b)** The assistant showed Mia lots of pretty shirts. **c)** The professor explained the meaning of the poem to the students. **d)** Did he say anything to you about the new neighbours?

6.

a) He made her very happy. **b)** I find the book on 1913 interesting. **c)** I always thought of our relationship as natural/I have always thought of our relationship as natural. **d)** The club elected Carter chairman. **e)** He regarded his election as a matter of course.

7.

a) out of, **b)** up with, **c)** out for, **d)** out of, **e)** down on, **f)** forward to, **g)** away with

22. Gebrauch des Passivs

1.

a) D, **b)** A, **c)** B, **d)** C

2.

a) was, **b)** was being, **c)** are going to be awarded, **d)** would you be, **e)** have been being

3.

a), **b)**, **d)**

4.

a) A new album has finally been released by Phil Collins. **b)** You might be seen! **c)** The school cafeteria is being refitted this term. **d)** The news will be made public by the British government as soon as possible. **e)** The sailing club was founded 40 years ago.

5.

a) will be, **b)** will be, **c)** were, **d)** would, **e)** Will, **f)** would be, **g)** will

6.

a) sind geschlossen, **b)** werden geschlossen, **c)** wurde gefasst, **d)** war repariert

7.

a) The children were looked after by our parents. **b)** Last week two houses in our road were broken into/Two houses in our road were broken into last week. **c)** Cookies were given only to the children.

8.

a) Vitamins are supposed to be good for us. **b)** He is said to have received the prize undeservedly. **c)** The epidemic is reported to have started in West Africa. **d)** She is believed to cheat in exams.

23. Gebrauch des Infinitivs

1.

a) B, **b)** C, **c)** A, **d)** E, **e)** G, **f)** D, **g)** I, **h)** F, **i)** H

2.

a) B, **b)** A, **c)** C, **d)** B

3.

Infinitiv ohne to: You may, Mr Butcher made me, She saw him, She would never, My parents let me, Did you hear them
Infinitiv mit to: The fireman warned us, I don't know what, The doctor advised him, You told her, Mary would like, Grandma wants, This is too much for me, Tom will be the first one

4.

a) happened to, **b)** don't seem to, **c)** am/'m likely to, **d)** appear to

5.

a) I don't want you to leave. **b)** The athletes wanted the spectators to cheer them on. **c)** Oliver asked him to step aside. **d)** I need him to do me a big favour. **e)** Harry expected her to go on a date with him. **f)** I didn't expect him to tell me the truth.

6.

a) ... where to find a cash machine? **b)** ... to buy for the new school year. **c)** ... (in order) to get the best view.

7.

a) As always, heavy traffic is to be expected before Christmas. **b)** Jenna's just posted some photos. She seems to be enjoying her trip to Italy. **c)** There's no food left. You should/ought to have come earlier. **d)** Alex must have missed the train. **e)** She decided not to ask him after all.

8.

a) F, **b)** C, **c)** D, **d)** A, **e)** B, **f)** E

9.

Infinitiv: to ask, to be sorry, to mean, to want;
ing-Form: to enjoy, to mind, to insist on, to look forward to, to be afraid of;
Infinitiv oder ing-Form: to try, to stop, to like

10.

a) get, **b)** sacrifice, **c)** discuss, **d)** meeting, **e)** cleaning, **f)** wanting, **g)** smoking, **h)** playing, **i)** complaining

24. Gebrauch des Gerund

1.

gerund: a), d), e),
kein gerund: b), c), f), g)

2.

a) Eating in unknown restaurants can be disappointing. (S), **b)** Some friends of mine love dancing the tango. (O), **c)** Shopping for clothes with one's husband may be a challenge. (S), **d)** I enjoy sailing. (O), **e)** Having to write dozens of christmas cards is rather stressful. (S)

3.

a) think of/about, **b)** succeed in, **c)** dream of, **d)** worry about, **e)** insist on, **f)** complain about, **g)** rely on, **h)** talk of/about, **i)** look forward to, **j)** danger of, **k)** idea of, **l)** be good/bad at, **m)** way of, **n)** be proud of, **o)** be interested in, **p)** difficulty in, **q)** be crazy about, **r)** be ashamed of

4.

a) <u>Sailing</u> is relaxing. **b)** <u>Ballet dancing</u> is our daughter's biggest hobby. **c)** I'm interested in <u>learning</u> an instrument. **d)** My husband prefers <u>drinking</u> coffee in the morning. **e)** I love <u>reading</u> in the evening.

5.

a) Dad wants Chris to go to a dog school with his dog. **b)** I didn't expect him to become so angry. **c)** He's tired of you barking all day long, Wolfie.

6.

<u>Bedeutungsunterschied</u>: a), c)

7.

a) feeding, **b)** to train, **c)** to keep, **d)** knowing, **e)** to be, **f)** complaining, **g)** to hang, **h)** giving, **i)** to refuse

25. Gebrauch von Partizipien

1.

a) H, **b)** C, **c)** G, **d)** E, **e)** I, **f)** D, **g)** J, **h)** B, **i)** A, **j)** F

2.

a) The children watched the new neighbours moving in. **b)** I always hear old Mrs Miller talking on the telephone. **c)** Have you seen Mr Butcher trimming the hedge? **d)** Did you notice the police helicopter circling yesterday?

3.

a) Wir standen Ewigkeiten draußen vor dem Club und warteten. **b)** Ein niedlicher Hund kam und schnüffelte an mir. **c)** Die Holzscheite liegen aufgestapelt hinter dem Haus. **d)** Die Straßen bleiben bei dieser Temperatur schneebedeckt.

4.

a) C, **b)** D, **c)** B, **d)** A, **e)** F, **f)** E

5.

a) has his hair cut, **b)** makes Dad carry out, **c)** let me keep, **d)** get them repaired, **e)** had everything delivered

6.

a) The girl <u>waiting</u> at the bus stop is one of my daughter's friends. **b)** <u>Looking</u> down from the plane, we saw the lights of the city below. **c)** While <u>staying</u> in London, I met one of my old friends from university. **d)** The guide led the way to the bus, the tourists <u>following</u> with their souvenirs. **e)** With winter <u>coming</u> fast, Chris has stopped cycling to work.

Wortliste

A

	... **a day**	... *pro Tag*
	a few	*ein paar*
	a lot of	*viel*
	about (adverb/preposition)	*ungefähr; über*
	abstract	*abstrakt*
	academic	*akademisch*
	accident	*Unfall; Zufall*
	according to (preposition)	*nach, zufolge, laut; entsprechend*
to	**achieve**	*etwas erreichen*
	across (adverb/ preposition)	*über + Dativ, jenseits, auf der anderen Seite*
	additional	*zusätzlich*
to	**admire**	*bewundern*
	advice	*Ratschlag*
to	**advise somebody to do something**	*jdm. raten, etwas zu tun*
to	**afford**	*sich etwas leisten*
	after (preposition/adverb)	*nach*
	afternoon	*Nachmittag*
	afterwards (adverb)	*danach*
	again	*wieder*
	ages (pl.)	*eine Ewigkeit, Ewigkeiten, ewig*
	ago (adverb)	*vor + Zeitangabe*
to	**agree on**	*(sich) einigen auf*
	alarm clock	*Wecker*
	alive	*lebendig*
	all	*ganze(r,s); alle(s)*
	all day long	*den ganzen Tag (lang)*
	all of	*den/die/das ganze(n)*
	all over	*komplett, ganz und gar; noch einmal*
	all the time	*die ganze Zeit*
	almost (adverb)	*fast*
	already (adverb)	*schon*
	alright	*in Ordnung*
	also (adverb)	*auch*
	although	*obwohl*
	always (adverb)	*immer*
	ambitious	*ehrgeizig*
	angry	*wütend, ärgerlich*
	animal	*Tier*
	annoyed	*verärgert*
	another	*ein/e andere(r,s)*
	any	*irgendein/-welche(r,s)*
	anything	*irgendetwas; ein, eine*
	anywhere	*irgendwo(hin)*
to	**apologize**	*sich entschuldigen*
to	**appear to**	*anscheinend ...*
	appointment	*Termin*
	area	*Bereich; Gegend*
to	**argue**	*streiten*
	argument	*Argument*
	around (preposition)	*gegen*
	as	*da, weil; wie*
	as ... as	*so ... wie*
	as of	*Stand am* (Datum)
	as well	*auch*
to	**ask for**	*fragen nach, bitten um*
to	**ask out** somebody	*jemanden* (auf einen Drink/ zum Essen) *einladen*
to	**ask** somebody **a favour**	*jdn. um einen Gefallen bitten*
	assembly	*Versammlung*
	at	*an*
	at once	*sofort*
	at one's place	*bei jdm. zuhause*
	at the moment	*jetzt, gerade*
	at this rate	*unter diesen Umständen*
	athlete	*Athlet(in), Sportler(in)*
	aunt	*Tante*
	automatically (adverb)	*automatisch*
to	**award** somebody **a prize**	*jdm. einen Preis verleihen*
	away (adj./adverb)	*weg, unterwegs*

B

	B.C., before Christ	*vor Christus*
to	**backslide, -slid, -slid**	*rückläufig sein; rückfällig werden*
	bad (adj.)	*schlecht*
	badly (adverb)	*schlimm*
	badminton	*Federball*
	ballet dancing	*Ballett tanzen, der Balletttanz*
	barely (adverb)	*kaum*
to	**bark**	*bellen*
	bathroom	*Badezimmer*
to	**batter**	*verbeulen*
	battered	*verbeult*
to	**be able to**	*können*
to	**be afraid of**	*vor jdm./etwas Angst haben*
to	**be allowed to**	*dürfen*
to	**be angry with** somebody	*jemandem böse sein*
to	**be ashamed of**	*sich für etwas schämen*
to	**be concerned**	*besorgt/betroffen sein*
to	**be crazy about**	*verrückt nach etwas sein*

to **be due**	*fällig sein, erwartet werden, ankommen sollen*
to **be fond of** + ing-form	*etwas gern tun*
to **be for sure**	*sicher sein*
to **be fun**	*Spaß machen*
to **be going to**	*werden*
to **be good/bad at**	*etwas gut/schlecht können*
to **be interested in**	*an etwas interessiert sein*
to **be jealous of** somebody	*neidisch auf jdn. sein*
to **be late**	*zu spät kommen, sich verspäten*
to **be likely to**	*wahrscheinlich sein*
to **be meant to**	*sein sollen*
to **be obliged to**	*verpflichtet sein*
to **be off**	*abgesagt sein, nicht mehr auf dem Programm stehen*
to **be proud of**	*stolz auf etwas sein*
to **be right**	*Recht haben*
to **be said to**	*angeblich sein sollen*
to **be sick of** something	*etwas leid sein, genug von etwas haben*
to **be sorry**	*leid tun*
to **be supposed to**	*sollte*
to **be sure about** something	*sich bei etwas sicher sein*
to **be tired**	*müde sein*
to **be tired of**	*genug von etwas haben*
to **be upset**	*aufgeregt sein*
to **be used to**	*daran gewöhnt sein*
to **be, was/were, been**	*sein*
beach	*Strand*
to **beat, beat, beaten**	*schlagen*
because	*weil*
to **become, became, become**	*werden*
before	*vor* + Dativ; *zuvor, vorher*
to **begin, began, begun**	*beginnen, anfangen*
to **behave**	*benehmen*
behind (preposition)	*hinter*
to **believe**	*glauben, denken*
bell	*Glocke*
to **belong**	*gehören*
below (preposition)	*unten; darunter*
best wishes	*beste Wünsche*
to **bet, bet/betted, bet/betted**	*wetten*
to **betray**	*verraten*
better	*besser*
biggest	*größte(r,s)*
bike	*Fahrrad; Motorrad*
bill	*Rechnung*
a **bit**	*ein bisschen, ein wenig*
to **bite, bit, bitten**	*beißen*
to **blame**	*Schuld geben*
blanket	*Decke*
to **block** something	*etwas blockieren*
to **blow, blew, blown**	*wehen, blasen, pusten*
book	*Buch*
to **borrow**	*sich etwas borgen/ausleihen (von jdm.)*
bottom	*Boden; (unteres) Ende*
to **brake**	*bremsen*
brake	*Bremse*
break	*Pause*
to **break into**	*einbrechen*
to **bring up**	*etwas zur Sprache bringen*
to **bring, brought, brought**	*bringen*
broken	*kaputt, zerbrochen*
brother	*Bruder*
bull	*Bulle, Stier*
to **bully somebody**	*jdn. schikanieren/mobben/drangsalieren*
burning	*brennend*
to **bury**	*beerdigen*
bus stop	*Bushaltestelle*
busy	*arbeitsreich; beschäftigt*
to **buy, bought, bought**	*kaufen*
by (any) chance	*durch (irgendeinen) Zufall*
by (preposition)	*bis*
by the time ...	*bis ...*

C

cake	*Kuchen*
call	*Anruf*
to **call** somebody **back**	*jdn. zurückrufen*
can (modal verb)	*können*
capacity	*Fähigkeit; Volumen*
car race	*Autorennen*
to **care for**	*sorgen für*
careful	*vorsichtig*
to **carry**	*tragen*
case	*Fall*
cash machine	*Geldautomat, Bankomat*
cat	*Katze*
catamaran	*Katamaran*
to **catch, caught, caught**	*fangen*
to **cause**	*verursachen*
to **celebrate**	*feiern*
certainly (adverb)	*sicherlich*

Wortliste

chairman	*Vorsitzender*
challenge	*Herausforderung*
chance	*Möglichkeit*
to **change**	*ändern; wechseln*
change	*Wandel*
charity	*Barmherzigkeit, Wohlfahrtsverband*
to **chat**	*plaudern, sich unterhalten; chatten*
to **cheat on** somebody	*jdn. betrügen*
to **check**	*prüfen*
child, children	*Kind, Kinder*
to **choose**	*auswählen*
christmas card	*Weihnachtskarte*
christmas cookies	*Weihnachtskekse*
Christmas Eve	*Heiligabend*
to **circle**	*kreisen*
class trip	*Klassenfahrt*
to **clean (up)**	*reinigen, putzen; aufräumen*
clear	*klar*
to **clear up**	*aufräumen*
to **climb**	*klettern*
to **close**	*schließen*
close	*nah*
cloudy	*wolkig, bewölkt*
coach	*Reisebus*
to **come across**	*(zufällig) auf etwas stoßen*
to **come back**	*zurückkommen*
to **come in**	*hereinkommen*
to **come, came, come**	*kommen*
to **compare**	*vergleichen*
competition	*Wettbewerb*
to **complain (about)**	*sich beschweren (über)*
to **complete**	*fertigstellen*
to **concentrate on**	*sich konzentrieren auf*
to **conclude**	*enden*
to **confine**	*beschränken; einsperren*
to **consider**	*in Betracht ziehen, berücksichtigen*
considerate	*rücksichtsvoll, aufmerksam*
to **contact somebody**	*jdn. kontaktieren*
to **continue**	*etwas weiterhin tun*
continuously (adverb)	*ständig*
contract	*Vertrag*
to **control**	*steuern, leiten, regulieren*
to **cook**	*kochen*
cookie	*Keks*
corner	*Ecke*
to **cost, cost, cost**	*kosten*
couch	*Couch, Sofa*
could	*könnte; konnte*
to **count**	*zählen*
to **count on**	*sich verlassen auf, darauf zählen*
couple	*Paar*
a **couple of**	*ein paar*
to **cover**	*zudecken, abdecken*
covered	*bedeckt*
to **create**	*schaffen*
to **criticize**	*kritisieren*
crowd	*(Menschen-)Menge*
cupcake	*kleiner verzierter Kuchen*
to **cut off**	*abschneiden; unterbrechen*
to **cut, cut, cut**	*schneiden*
cute	*niedlich*
to **cycle**	*radeln, radfahren*

D

to **damage**	*beschädigen*
damage	*Schaden*
dancing	*tanzend*
danger	*Gefahr*
darker	*dunkler*
daughter	*Tochter*
death	*Tod*
decade	*Jahrzehnt*
to **decide**	*sich entscheiden*
decision	*Entscheidung*
to **deliver**	*liefern*
dentist	*Zahnarzt, -ärztin*
dessert	*Dessert, Nachtisch*
to **develop**	*entwickeln*
dictionary	*Wörterbuch*
to **die**	*sterben*
different	*unterschiedlich, verschieden*
difficult	*schwierig, schwer*
difficulty	*Schwierigkeit*
dignified	*würdig, würdevoll*
dinner	*(Mittag-/Abend-)Essen*
to **disappoint**	*enttäuschen*
to **discover**	*entdecken*
to **discuss**	*diskutieren*
to **dislike**	*nicht mögen*
to **disqualify**	*disqualifizieren*
distraction	*Ablenkung*
to **disturb**	*stören*

to **dive**	*tauchen*
to **do well**	*gut gehen*
to **do/does, did, done**	*tun*
dog school	*Hundeschule*
doll	*Puppe*
doll's house	*Puppenhaus*
to **donate**	*spenden*
dozens of	*Dutzende (von)*
draught	*Zug(luft)*
to **dream of**	*träumen von*
to **drive off**	*wegfahren*
to **drive past**	*vorbeifahren*
to **drive, drove, driven**	*(selbst) fahren*
driver	*Fahrer(in)*
during (preposition)	*während*
dusk	*Abenddämmerung*
dustbin	*Mülleimer*

E

each	*jede(r,s) einzelne(r,s)*
each other	*sich (gegenseitig)*
earlier	*früher*
early (adj./adverb)	*früh*
to **eat, ate, eaten**	*essen*
effect	*Auswirkung, Effekt*
elderly	*ältere(r,s)*
to **elect somebody**	*jemanden wählen*
embarrassing	*peinlich, beschämend*
emergency	*Notfall*
to **emigrate**	*auswandern*
to **empty**	*leeren*
to **encourage somebody to do something**	*jdn. ermutigen, etwas zu tun*
to **enjoy**	*genießen*
to **enlarge**	*vergrößern*
enough	*genug*
envelope	*Umschlag*
epidemic	*Epidemie*
essay	*Aufsatz, Essay*
evening	*Abend*
ever	*jemals*
every	*jede(r,s)*
everything	*alles*
everywhere	*überall*
exam	*Prüfung*
to **examine**	*untersuchen*
to **exchange**	*tauschen, austauschen*
exciting	*aufregend*
to **exhaust**	*anstrengen*
exhibition	*Ausstellung*
to **expand**	*zunehmen, wachsen, sich/etwas erweitern, ausdehnen*
to **expect**	*erwarten*
experience	*Erfahrung*
to **explain**	*erklären*
to **extinguish**	*löschen*

F

to **face**	*gegenübertreten*
to **fail**	*scheitern; durchfallen*
to **fall off**	*herunterfallen*
to **fall pregnant**	*(unbeabsichtigt) schwanger werden*
to **fall, fell, fallen**	*fallen*
fascinating	*faszinierend*
fast	*schnell*
favour	*Gefallen*
favourite	*Lieblings-*
to **feed**	*füttern*
to **feel, felt, felt**	*fühlen*
to **fell**	*fällen*
to **fight, fought, fought**	*kämpfen*
to **fill in for somebody**	*für jdn. einspringen*
final exam	*Abschlussprüfung*
finally (adverb)	*schließlich, endlich*
to **find, found, found**	*finden*
to **finish**	*beenden*
fire door	*Feuerschutztür*
firefighter	*Feuerwehrmann/-frau*
fireman, -men	*Feuerwehrmann/-männer*
firewood	*Feuerholz*
first	*erste; zuerst*
to **fit, fit, fit**	*passen* (Größe)
to **fix**	*reparieren*
flat	*flach*
flight	*Flug*
flute	*Flöte*
to **fly, flew, flown**	*fliegen*
to **follow**	*folgen*
for	*für; seit; wegen*
for ages	*eine Ewigkeit, Ewigkeiten, ewig*
for sure	*bestimmt, ganz sicher*
forbidden	*verboten*
to **forecast**	*vorhersagen*
forever	*für immer*

Wortliste

to **forget, forgot, forgotten**	*vergessen*
to **forgive, forgave, forgiven**	*vergeben, verzeihen*
form teacher	*Klassenlehrer(in)*
fortieth	*vierzigste(r,s)*
freezing	*eiskalt*
friendly (adjective)	*freundlich*
fuel	*Treibstoff, Benzin*
funny	*lustig*
furniture	*Möbel*
future	*Zukunft*

G

game	*Spiel*
gap	*Lücke*
gap year	*freies Jahr* (z. B. zwischen Schule und Studienantritt)
garage	*Garage; Werkstatt*
garden party	*Gartenparty*
geography	*Erdkunde*
to **get dressed**	*sich anziehen*
to **get into** something	*(in etwas) einsteigen*
to **get off**	*aussteigen*
to **get on** somebody's **nerves**	*jdm. auf die Nerven gehen*
to **get on with**	*zurechtkommen mit*
to **get over**	*hinwegkommen über*
to **get** something **done**	*etwas machen lassen*
to **get up**	*aufstehen*
to **get, got, got**	*bekommen*
to **give (gave, given)** something to somebody	*jdm. etwas geben*
to **give up**	*aufgeben*
glasses (pl.)	*Brille*
to **go on** + ing-form	*etwas weiterhin tun*
to **go on holiday**	*in Urlaub fahren*
to **go, went, gone**	*gehen*
good	*gut*
goodbye	*auf Wiedersehen*
government	*Regierung*
great	*großartig; groß*
Greek	*griechisch; Grieche, Griechin, Griechen*
to **groom**	*bürsten, Fell pflegen*
to **grow, grew, grown**	*wachsen*
to **guess**	*raten*
guide	*Touristenführer(in)*
guitar	*Gitarre*

H

half	*Hälfte*
half an hour	*halbe Stunde*
to **happen**	*passieren, geschehen*
to **happen to do** something	*zufällig etwas tun*
happiness	*Glück*
harbour	*Hafen*
hard	*hart; schwierig, schwer; anstrengend*
hardly (adverb)	*kaum*
hat	*Hut*
to **hate**	*hassen*
to **have a baby**	*ein Baby bekommen*
to **have a good time**	*eine schöne Zeit haben/verbringen*
to **have fun**	*Spaß haben*
to **have** something	*etwas zu sich nehmen*
to **have** something **done**	*etwas tun/machen lassen*
to **have to**	*müssen*
to **have, had, had**	*haben*
he (pronoun)	*er*
healthiest	*gesündeste(r,s)*
to **hear, heard, heard**	*hören*
heaven	*Himmel*
hedge	*Hecke*
to **help**	*helfen*
her (adjective)	*ihr*
her (pronoun)	*ihr, sie*
hers (possessive pronoun)	*ihr, ihre(r,s)*
herself (reflexive pronoun)	*sich selbst; sie (selbst)*
to **hide, hid, hidden**	*verstecken*
him (pronoun)	*ihn, ihm*
himself (refexive pronoun)	*sich selbst; er (selbst)*
his (possessive pronoun)	*sein, seine(r,s)*
to **hit, hit, hit**	*schlagen, treffen; jdm. aufgehen; stoßen auf*
to **hold on**	*warten; sich festhalten*
to **hold, held, held**	*(ab)halten*
home-made	*hausgemacht, selbstgemacht*
to **hope**	*hoffen*
how (adverb)	*wie*
How/What about … ?	*Wie wär's mit … ?*
however (adverb)	*jedoch*
huge	*riesig*
hungry	*hungrig*
to **hurry**	*sich beeilen*
husband	*Ehemann*

I

I (pronoun)	*ich*
ice cap	*Polarkappe*
ice-cream parlour	*Eisdiele*
Iceland	*Island*
idea	*Idee*
if (conjunction)	*wenn, falls*
ill	*krank*
to **imagine**	*sich (etwas) vorstellen*
to **import**	*importieren, einführen*
import	*Importware*
important	*wichtig*
to **improve something**	*etwas verbessern*
in front of (preposition)	*vor*
in person	*persönlich*
in term time	*während des Trimesters/ Semesters*
in the evening	*abends*
in time	*rechtzeitig*
including	*einschließlich*
to **increase**	*wachsen, steigen*
India	*Indien*
indoors (adverb)	*innen, drinnen*
to **inform**	*informieren*
injured	*verletzt*
inside (adverb/preposition)	*drinnen*
to **insist on**	*bestehen auf*
instead (adverb)	*stattdessen*
insurance	*Versicherung, Versicherungsbranche*
to **intend**	*beabsichtigen*
interest	*Interesse*
interested	*interessiert*
interesting	*interessant*
internet search engine	*Internetsuchmaschine*
to **interrupt**	*unterbrechen, stören*
to **introduce**	*vorstellen*
to **invite**	*einladen*
the **ironing**	*das Bügeln*
to **irritate**	*verärgern*
island	*Insel*
it (pronoun)	*es*
its (possessive pronoun)	*sein, seine(r,s), ihr, ihre(r,s)*
it's a pity ...	*es ist schade, dass ...*
it's no good ...	*es nützt nichts, ...*
it's no use ...	*es hat keinen Zweck*
it's worth ...	*es lohnt sich, ...*
itself (reflexive pronoun)	*sich, sich selbst, man selbst*

J

to **join** somebody	*jdm. Gesellschaft leisten, dazu-/nachkommen, dazusetzen*
to **joke**	*scherzen*
journey	*Reise*
just (adverb)	*gerade eben; nur*

K

to **keep doing something**	*etwas weiter tun*
to **keep one's promise**	*sein Versprechen halten*
to **keep somebody company**	*jdm. Gesellschaft leisten*
to **keep up with** somebody/ something	*mit jdm./etwas mithalten*
to **keep, kept, kept**	*halten, behalten*
key	*Schlüssel*
to **kill**	*töten*
kind of	*Art von*
to **kiss**	*küssen*
kitchen	*Küche*
kitten	*Kätzchen*
to **knock**	*klopfen*
to **know, knew, known**	*wissen, kennen*

L

Lake Constance	*Bodensee*
large	*groß*
last (adj./adverb)	*letzte/-r/-s; zuletzt*
lately (adverb)	*kürzlich, in letzter Zeit*
to **laugh**	*lachen*
lawn	*Rasen*
to **lay, laid, laid**	*legen*
lazy	*faul*
to **lead, led, led**	*führen*
to **lean back**	*zurücklehnen*
to **lean, leant/leaned, leant/leaned**	*sich lehnen/beugen*
to **learn, learnt/learned, learnt/learned**	*lernen*
leash	*Leine*
to **leave somebody alone**	*jdn. in Ruhe lassen; jdn. allein lassen*
to **leave, left, left**	*verlassen, abreisen*
to **lend (lent, lent)** somebody something	*jdm. etwas leihen*
lesson	*Schulstunde*
to **let (let, let)** somebody do something	*zulassen, dass jemand etwas tut*

Wortliste

to **let somebody down**	*jdn. im Stich lassen*
let's	*lass(t) uns*
letter	*Brief*
to **lie**	*lügen*
to **lie, lay, lain**	*liegen*
light	*Licht*
lightning	*Blitz*
like (preposition/ conjunction)	*wie*
to **listen to the radio**	*Radio hören*
to **live**	*leben, wohnen*
living-room	*Wohnzimmer*
local	*örtlich*
to **lock**	*abschließen*
locked	*abgeschlossen*
log	*Holzscheit*
to **log on to**	*sich einloggen bei/auf*
logically (adverb)	*logisch*
to **look after** somebody/ something	*auf jdn./etwas aufpassen*
to **look down**	*herunterschauen*
to **look forward to** + ing-form	*sich freuen auf*
to **look over** something	*etwas durchsehen*
to **look up to** somebody	*zu jemandem aufschauen*
to **lose weight**	*abnehmen*
loss	*Verlust*
lots of (pronoun)	*viel(e), jede Menge*
to **love**	*lieben*
luggage	*Gepäck*
lunch	*Mittagessen*

M

magazine	*Zeitschrift*
major	*Haupt-*
to **make it**	*es schaffen*
to **make oneself at home**	*es sich bequem machen, sich wie zuhause fühlen*
to **make somebody do something**	*jemanden etwas machen lassen*
to **make, made, made**	*machen, tun*
to **manage**	hier: *etwas schaffen*
many (adjective/pronoun)	*viele*
married	*verheiratet*
to **marry**	*heiraten*
to **match**	*passen* (farblich)
match	*Spiel*
a **matter of**	*eine Sache des ...*
a **matter of course**	*Selbstverständlichkeit*
may (modal verb)	*können, dürfen*
me (pronoun)	*mich, mir*
me (pronoun)	*mich; mir*
to **mean**	*beabsichtigen*
meat	*Fleisch*
mechanic	*Mechaniker(in)*
to **meet, met, met**	*treffen*
to **melt**	*schmelzen*
memory	*Erinnerung*
to **mention**	*erwähnen*
mess	*Unordnung*
message	*Nachricht*
midday	*Mittag*
might (modal verb)	*könnte (vielleicht)*
to **mind**	*beachten*
mine (possessive pronoun)	*mein, meine(r,s)*
mine (pronoun)	*meine, meiner, meins; von mir*
mirror	*Spiegel*
to **mislead (-led, -led)** somebody	*jdn. täuschen*
to **miss**	*vermissen; verpassen*
mistake	*Fehler*
to **mob**	*umringen*
mobile (phone)	*Mobiltelefon*
money	*Geld*
month	*Monat*
more (adjective/pronoun)	*mehr*
morning paper	*Morgenzeitung*
mosquito, -(e)s	*Mücke, Mücken*
mostly (adverb)	*meist*
mountain	*Berg*
to **move**	*bewegen; umziehen*
to **move in**	*einziehen*
to **mow**	*mähen*
much (adjective/ pronoun/adverb)	*viel*
mud puddle	*Schlammpfütze*
must (modal verb)	*müssen*
my (adjective)	*mein, meine(r,s)*
myself (reflexive pronoun)	*mir/mich; ich selbst*

N

near (adjective/adverb/ preposition)	*nahe, in der Nähe von, bei*
necessary	*notwendig, nötig*
need (modal verb)	*brauchen*
neighbour	*Nachbar(in)*
neither ... nor (adverb/ conjunction)	*weder ... noch*
never (adverb)	*niemals*
news	*Neuigkeiten; Nachrichten*

nobody (pronoun)	*niemand*
noise	*Lärm, Geräusch*
non-stop	*ununterbrochen, nonstop*
nor (adverb/conjunction)	*und ... auch nicht, noch*
nostalgic	*nostalgisch*
not any more	*nicht mehr*
not yet	*noch nicht*
note	*Banknote*
to **notice**	*bemerken*
now (adverb)	*jetzt*
nowhere (adverb)	*nirgends*

O

to **object to**	*etwas dagegen haben*
to **observe**	*beobachten, bemerken*
occupation	*Beschäftigung*
oddly (adverb)	*seltsam*
of course	*natürlich*
to **offend**	*verärgern*
to **offer**	*anbieten*
often (adverb)	*oft*
old	*alt*
old people's home	*Seniorenheim*
old town	*Altstadt*
old-fashioned	*altmodisch*
on the run	*auf der Flucht*
on the telephone	*am Telefon*
on time	*pünktlich*
once (adverb)	*einmal*
one (adjective/pronoun)	*ein, eine*
oneself (reflexive pronoun)	*sich selbst, man selbst*
to **open**	*öffnen*
other (adjective/pronoun)	*andere(r,s)*
ought to (modal verb)	*sollte*
our (adjective)	*unser, unsere(r,s)*
ours (possessive pronoun)	*unser, unsere(r,s)*
ourselves (reflexive pronoun)	*uns, uns selbst*
outside (adverb)	*draußen*
outstanding	*herausragend*
oven	*Ofen*
over (adverb)	*vorbei*
over (preposition)	*über; in; während*
to **overhear**	*zufällig mithören*
to **overlook**	*übersehen*
to **oversee, -saw, -seen**	*beaufsichtigen*
to **overtake**	*überholen*
owner	*Eigentümer(in)*

P

to **paint**	*malen, streichen*
to **participate in**	*teilnehmen an*
to **pass on**	*weitergeben, -reichen*
to **pass** somebody **over to** somebody	*jdn. weiterverbinden*
to **pat**	*tätscheln*
to **pay attention**	*Acht geben, aufpassen*
to **pay, paid, paid**	*bezahlen*
penpal	*Brieffreund(in)*
people	*Leute*
perfect	*perfekt*
to **perform**	*aufführen*
performance	*Leistung*
period	*Schulstunde*
permission	*Erlaubnis*
to **persuade**	*überreden*
piano lessons	*Klavierstunden*
to **pick somebody up**	*jdn. abholen*
to **pick up**	*abnehmen* (Telefon)
picture	*Bild*
plane	*(Verkehrs)Flugzeug*
plant	*Pflanze*
to **play**	*spielen*
play	*Theaterstück*
please	*bitte*
pocket money	*Taschengeld*
police helicopter	*Polizeihubschrauber*
to **populate**	*bevölkern*
porridge	*Porridge, Haferbrei*
to **practice**	*üben*
to **pray**	*beten*
to **predict**	*vorhersagen*
to **prefer**	*bevorzugen*
to **prepare**	*vorbereiten*
present	*Geschenk*
president	*Präsident(in)*
press coverage	*Berichterstattung* (in der Presse)
pretzel	*Brezel*
price	*Preis* (Kosten)
primary school	*Grundschule*
prize	*Preis* (Gewinn)
probably (adverb)	*wahrscheinlich*
to **promise**	*versprechen*
properly (adverb)	*richtig, ordentlich*
to **propose**	*vorschlagen*

Wortliste

to **prove**	*beweisen*
to **provoke**	*provozieren; hervorrufen*
public	*öffentlich*
public transport	*öffentlicher Nahverkehr*
to **pull out of something**	*sich aus etwas zurückziehen, aus etwas aussteigen*
punctual	*pünktlich*
to **purr**	*schnurren*
to **put away**	*aufräumen*
to **put on**	*auflegen; anziehen*
to **put out**	*hinausstellen*
to **put, put, put**	*setzen, stellen, legen*
pyjamas	*Schlafanzug*

Q

to **quarrel**	*sich streiten*
the **Queen**	*die englische Königin*
queen	*Königin*
question tag	*Frageanhängsel*
quietly (adverb)	*still, ruhig*
to **quit, quit, quit**	*aufhören; kündigen*
quite (adverb)	*ziemlich; ganz, völlig*

R

railway station	*Bahnhof*
rain	*Regen*
to **raise**	*(an)heben, erhöhen*
rarely (adverb)	*selten*
rather (adverb)	*eher; ziemlich*
to **reach**	*jdn./etwas erreichen*
to **react**	*reagieren*
to **read, read, read**	*lesen*
ready (adjective)	*fertig, bereit*
real (adjective)	*echte(r,s)*
to **realise**	*erkennen, begreifen, sich (einer Sache) bewusst sein/werden*
really (adverb)	*wirklich, richtig*
rear light	*Rücklicht*
to **receive**	*erhalten, bekommen*
recent (adjective)	*kürzlich; neueste(r,s), jüngste(r,s)*
recently (adverb)	*kürzlich*
receptionist	*Rezeptionist(in); Sprechstundenhilfe*
to **reclaim**	*zurückverlangen, zurückfordern*
to **recommend**	*empfehlen*
referee	*Schiedsrichter*
to **refit**	*überholt werden, neu ausstatten*
to **refuse**	*sich weigern*
to **regard** something **as** something	*etwas als ... betrachten/ansehen*
to **regret**	*bedauern*
regularly (adverb)	*regelmäßig*
relationship	*Beziehung*
relaxed	*entspannt*
to **release**	*veröffentlichen*
to **rely on**	*sich verlassen auf*
to **remain**	*bleiben*
to **remember**	*sich erinnern, daran denken*
to **remind** somebody **of** something	*jdn. an etwas erinnern*
to **repaint**	*neu anstreichen*
repellent	*Abwehrmittel*
to **replace**	*ersetzen*
to **reply**	*antworten*
to **report**	*berichten*
report	*Bericht*
to **request** something	*um etwas bitten*
to **rescue**	*retten*
to **resend, -sent, -sent**	*erneut senden*
to **reset, -set, -set**	(Uhr) *neu stellen,* (Computer) *neu starten*
to **respect**	*respektieren*
result	*Ergebnis*
to **revise**	(den Stoff) *wiederholen*
rich (adjective)	*reich*
to **ride, rode, ridden**	*reiten*
riding school	*Reitschule*
right (adjective)	*richtige*
right now	*im Moment*
to **ring, rang, rung**	*klingeln; anrufen*
to **rise, rose, risen**	*steigen; aufgehen; sich erheben*
road	*Straße*
rocking horse	*Schaukelpferd*
to **row**	*rudern*
to **row**	*sich streiten*
row	*Streit; Lärm*
row	*Reihe*
rowing trip	*Ruderausflug*
rubbish	*Müll*
to **ruin**	*ruinieren, kaputtmachen*
rule	*Regel*
run-down (adjective)	hier: *heruntergeritten; heruntergekommen*

S

to **sacrifice**	*opfern*
safe (adjective)	*sicher*
sailing	*Segeln*
sailing club	*Segelverein*
same (adjective/ pronoun/adverb)	*gleiche(r,s)*
to **saw, sawed, sawn**	*sägen*
scarcely (adverb)	*kaum*
to **scratch**	*etwas zerkratzen*
screen	*Bildschirm*
sea	*Meer*
seat	*Sitz(platz)*
second	*Sekunde*
secret	*Geheimnis*
to **seem to**	*scheinbar ...*
seldom (adverb)	*selten*
to **sell, sold, sold**	*verkaufen*
set	*Reihe*
to **set, set, set a timescale**	*einen Zeitplan festlegen*
several (adjective/ pronoun)	*einige, verschiedene; jeweilige; ein paar*
shall (modal verb)	*sollen*
she (pronoun)	*sie*
shelf, shelves	*Regal, Regale*
shoe	*Schuh*
should (modal verb)	*sollte*
to **shout**	*rufen*
to **show, showed, shown**	*zeigen*
shutters (pl.)	*Rolladen*
sick (adjective)	*krank; übel*
sights (pl.)	*Sehenswürdigkeiten*
sightseeing	*Besichtigungen*
to **sign**	*unterschreiben*
since (preposition/ conjunction)	*seit*
sister	*Schwester*
to **sit down**	*sich hinsetzen*
to **sit, sat, sat**	*sitzen*
site	*Website*
sky	*Himmel*
to **sleep,slept, slept**	*schlafen*
sleeping	*schlafend*
slice	*Scheibe*
small (adjective)	*klein*
to **smash**	*zerschlagen*
smiling	*lächelnd*
to **sniff**	*schnüffeln*
to **snow**	*schneien*
so (adverb/conjunction)	*auch* (in Kurzsätzen wie "So am I." - "Ich auch.")
so far	*bis jetzt*
society	*Gesellschaft*
some (adjective/pronoun)	*etwas, einige*
somebody/somewhere else (pronoun)	*jemand/irgendwo anders*
sometimes (adverb)	*manchmal*
soon (adverb)	*bald*
to **sound**	*klingen*
souvenir	*Souvenir, Reiseandenken*
to **spare**	*verschonen*
to **speak, spoke, spoken**	*sprechen*
species (sg. + pl.)	*Art, Spezies*
spectator	*Zuschauer(in)*
speech	*Rede*
to **spell, spelled/spelt, spelled/spelt**	*buchstabieren*
to **spend, spent, spent**	*verbringen*
spider	*Spinne*
stable	*Stall*
to **stack**	*stapeln*
stadium	*Stadion*
stain	*Fleck*
to **stand up for**	*sich einsetzen für*
to **stand, stood, stood**	*stehen*
to **start**	*anfangen*
station	*Bahnhof*
to **stay**	*bleiben, übernachten*
to **stay up**	*aufbleiben*
to **steal, stole, stolen**	*stehlen*
to **steer**	*lenken, manövrieren*
to **step**	*treten*
still (adverb)	*immer noch*
storm	*Sturm*
story	*Geschichte*
straight (adjective/adverb)	*gerade(wegs)*
street	*Straße*
stressful (adjective)	*stressig*
to **strike, struck, struck**	*schlagen*
to **stroke**	*streicheln*
strong (adjective)	*stark*
to **struggle**	*kämpfen*
to **study**	*studieren, lernen*
to **succeed in**	*etwas mit Erfolg tun*
suddenly (adverb)	*plötzlich*
to **suit**	*passen, stehen*

Wortliste

suit	*Anzug*
summer	*Sommer*
summer job	*Sommerferienjob*
to **suppose**	*annehmen*
sure (adjective/adverb)	*sicher*
survey	*Umfrage*
sweets (pl.)	*Süßigkeiten*
to **swing, swung, swung**	*schwingen, schaukeln*
to **switch on**	*einschalten*

T

to **take a call**	*einen Anruf entgegennehmen*
to **take care of** somebody/something	*sich um jdn./etwas kümmern*
to **take off**	*abheben*
to **take out**	*etwas herausnehmen; etwas hinausbringen; jemanden ausführen; (Essen) mitnehmen*
to **take over**	*übernehmen*
to **take** something **into account**	*etwas berücksichtigen*
to **take up**	*etwas anfangen/beginnen*
to **take, took, taken**	*(an)nehmen*
to **talk**	*sprechen*
to **talk about/of**	*darüber reden*
task	*Aufgabe*
to **taste**	*schmecken; probieren*
to **teach, taught, taught**	*unterrichten*
teacher	*Lehrer(in)*
temperature	*Temperatur; Fieber*
temporarily (adverb)	*zeitweise, vorübergehend*
to **tend to**	*neigen zu, sich kümmern um*
term	*Semester, Trimester*
than (preposition/conjunction)	*als (bei Vergleichen)*
Thank you for	*Danke für .../dafür, dass ...*
Thanksgiving	*amerikanisches Erntedankfest*
that (adjective/pronoun)	*der/die/das (dort/da); jene(r,s)*
the Caribbean	*die Karibik*
the Maldives	*die Malediven*
theatre	*Theater*
their (adjective)	*ihr* (Pl.)
theirs (possessive pronoun)	*ihr, ihre(r,s)* (Pl.)
them (pronoun)	*sie; ihnen*
themselves (reflexive pronoun)	*sie selbst*
then (adverb)	*dann*
there's no ...	*wörtlich: es gibt kein/keine(r,s)*
these days	*in letzter Zeit; heutzutage, heute, zurzeit*
they (pronoun)	*sie*
thief, -ves	*Dieb, Diebe*
thing	*Ding*
to **think about/of**	*darüber nachdenken/daran denken*
to **think something over**	*etwas überdenken*
this season	*diese Saison*
this time	*dieses Mal*
though (adverb/conjunction)	*jedoch; obwohl*
three	*drei*
through (preposition)	*durch*
to **throw, threw, thrown**	*werfen*
thump	*dumpfer Knall*
time	*Mal; Zeit*
to **tire**	*ermüden*
today (adverb)	*heute*
together (adverb)	*zusammen*
tomorrow (adverb)	*morgen*
tonight (adverb)	*heute Abend*
too (adverb)	*auch; zu* (+ Adjektiv)
top	*beste(r,s), oberste(r,s)*
totally (adverb)	*völlig, ganz*
to **touch**	*berühren*
tournament	*Turnier*
traffic	*Verkehr*
to **train**	*trainieren*
train	*Zug* (Bahn)
to **transfer to**	*versetzen nach*
to **travel**	*reisen*
to **trim**	*schneiden, zurechtstutzen*
trip	*Reise*
trouble	*Ärger*
to **trust in somebody**	*jemandem vertrauen*
truth	*Wahrheit*
to **try**	*versuchen*
try	*Versuch*
to **try hard to do something**	*sich sehr bemühen, etwas zu tun*
to **turn**	*drehen, umdrehen*
to **turn off**	*abschalten*
to **turn up**	*auftauchen, erscheinen*
twice (adverb)	*zweimal*

U

	UK, United Kingdom	*Vereinigtes Königreich*
	umbrella	*Regenschirm*
to	**undercut, -cut, -cut**	*unterbieten; untergraben*
to	**understand, understood, understood**	*verstehen*
	undeservedly (adverb)	*unverdientermaßen*
to	**unfold**	*aufschlagen*
	unfortunately (adverb)	*leider, unglücklicherweise*
	unknown (adjective)	*unbekannt*
	until (preposition/ conjunction)	*bis*
	unusual (adjective)	*ungewöhnlich*
	us (pronoun)	*uns*
to	**use**	*verwenden, nutzen*
	used to + infinitive	*früher/immer etwas getan haben*
	useful (adjective)	*sinnvoll, nützlich*
	usually (adverb)	*gewöhnlich*

V

	vaccination	*Impfung*
	vegetarian	*Vegetarier(in)*
	view	*Blick, Aussicht*
	village	*Dorf*
to	**visit**	*besuchen*

W

to	**wait for**	*warten auf*
	walking	*Geh-; wandelnd*
	wardrobe	*Garderobe*
to	**warm up**	*sich aufwärmen*
to	**warn**	*warnen*
	wash	*Wäsche*
	washing up	*Abwasch*
to	**watch**	*(an)schauen; beobachten*
to	**water**	*gießen, bewässern*
	way	*Weg; Art und Weise*
	we (pronoun)	*wir*
to	**wear, wore, worn**	*tragen* (Kleidung)
	weight	*Gewicht*
	well (adverb)	*gut*
	well done (adjective)	*gut gemacht*
	what (pronoun/ adjective/adverb)	*was*
	whatever (pronoun/ adjective/adverb)	*was (auch immer)*
	when (adverb)	*wann*
	when (conjunction)	*als; wenn*
	whenever (conjunction/ adverb)	*jedesmal wenn, wann auch immer*
	whether (conjunction)	*ob*
	which (pronoun/adjective)	*welche(r,n,s); der, die, das*
	while (conjunction)	*während*
	who (pronoun)	*wer; der-/diejenige(n), welche(r)*
	whole (adjective)	*ganze(r,s); alle(s)*
	why (adverb)	*warum*
	wife	*Ehefrau*
	will (modal verb)	*werden*
	wind	*Wind; Kurve*
to	**wind, wound, wound**	*aufziehen*
	wine	*Wein*
to	**wish**	*(sich/jemandem etwas) wünschen*
	with (preposition)	*mit*
	without (preposition)	*ohne*
to	**wonder**	*sich fragen*
to	**work**	*arbeiten*
	work	*Arbeit*
to	**worry**	*sich sorgen*
to	**worry about**	*sich Sorgen machen um*
	would (modal verb)	*würde*
	Would you mind ... ?	*Würde es Dir/Ihnen etwas ausmachen, ... ?*
to	**wound**	*verwunden*
	wound	*Wunde*

Y

yesterday (adverb)	*gestern*
yet (adverb/conjunction)	*schon*
you (pronoun)	*du; Sie*
you (pronoun)	*ihr; Sie* (Pl.)
you (pronoun)	*euch; Sie; Ihnen*
you (pronoun)	*dich; Sie; dir; Ihnen*
young (adjective)	*jung*
your (adjective)	*dein, Ihr*
your (adjective)	*euer, Ihr*
yours (possessive pronoun)	*dein, deine(r,s)*
yourself (reflexive pronoun)	*dir/dich, (Sie) sich (selbst)*
yourselves (reflexive pronoun)	*ihr/Sie* (Pl.) *selbst*

Bildnachweis

S. 29: A fotolia/ jörn buchheim, B shutterstock/ Mike Brake, C shutterstock/ auremar, D fotolia/ AVAVA; **S. 58:** a) fotolia/goodluz, b) fotolia/pressmaster , c) fotolia/Minerva Studio, d) fotolia/Alliance, e) fotolia/Martinan, f) fotolia/Chepko Danil; **S. 64:** a) thinkstockphotos/ istockphoto, A shutterstock/ Neale Cousland, b) fotolia/ Brocreative, B istockphoto/ Jeannot Olivet, c) thinkstockphotos/ BananaStock, C istockphoto/ alle12, d) istockphoto/ Wilson Valentin, D fotolia/ Janina Dierks; **S. 66** fotolia/Julija Sapic; **S. 71:** a) fotolia/EpicStockMedia, b) fotolia/grafikplusfoto, c) fotolia/Bastos, d) fotolia/S.Kobold; **S. 76:** a) fotolia/Kzenon, b) fotolia/Jenner, c) fotolia/petunyia, d) fotolia/ivan kmit, e) fotolia/contrastwerkstatt, f) fotolia/mimagephotos, g) fotolia/Click Images; **S. 78:** a) fotolia/Ana Blazic Pavlovic; b) fotolia/Francesco83, c) fotolia/Photographee.eu, d) fotolia/Kzenon; **S. 83:** a) fotolia/Thaut Images, A fotolia/Klaus The, c) fotolia/VRD, E fotolia/rdnzl, f) fotolia/Lorenz Timm, F fotolia/PhotographyByMK; **S. 89:** a) fotolia/Fabio Lotti, b) fotolia/Kathrin39, c) fotolia/Gina Sanders, d) fotolia/Aliaksei Lasevich, e) fotolia/Claudia Paulussen; **S. 93:** A fotolia/Photographee.eu, B fotolia/ACP prod, C fotolia/QQ7, D fotolia/natkamol; **S. 98:** a) fotolia/beawolf, b) fotolia/Ana Blazic Pavlovic, c) fotolia/ Sabphoto, d) fotolia/Robert Kneschke, e) fotolia/lefata; **S. 101:** a) fotolia/marqs, b) fotolia/contrastwerkstatt, c) fotolia/ mikelaptev, d) fotolia/autofocus67, e) fotolia/Kitty, f) fotolia/WavebreakMediaMicro, g) fotolia/stockWERK; **S. 117:** A shutterstock/ Zyankarlo; B shutterstock/ Andrey Arkusha, C shutterstock/ stocknadia, D shutterstock.com/Yuri Arcurs, E fotolia.de/ Ruth Black, F istock/ Viktor1, G fotolia/natkamol, H fotolia.de/ olly, I fotolia/ Oleg Kozlov, J shutterstock/ Iakov Filimonov; **S. 119:** a) fotolia/Amir Kaljikovic, b) fotolia/hitdelight, c) fotolia/Ammentorp, d) fotolia/Subbotina Anna, e) fotolia/Mariusz Prusaczyk, f) fotolia/Syda Productions